Acknowledgements:
The publishers wish to thank everybody who assisted in collecting the information and photographs contained in this book, particularly Mike Toy and Mike Seale. Thanks are also due to Clarence and Pamela Hiles for their advice and contribution to the text in the *Sporting Barbados* and *Where to Get Uncorked* features, as well as background research for the hotels and restaurant sections. Around the island many companies and individuals gave their time to ensure that this project was a success. In particular, we would like to thank Hamish Watson, the General Manager of the Cobbler's Cove Hotel and his delightful staff; National Car Rental; Trilicia Crawford and Captain Paul Archer at Bajan Helicopters; Andy Whiffen and his fantastic team at the Lone Star Restaurant; Lawrence E. Williams of L. E. Williams Tour Co. Ltd., Chris Trew at Best of Barbados Ltd; Mike Scantlebury, Hugh Foster and Brenda Edwards at the Barbados Tourism Authority; Dean Straker of the Plantation Restaurant and Garden Theatre; Neil and Nuru Patterson of Ragamuffin's; Sarah Carpenter and finally to the late Mohamed Amin, the inspiration behind the entire project.

First published in the UK by:
Cadogan Books plc
London House, Parkgate Road, London, SW11 4NQ, United Kingdom

In the USA by:
The Globe Pequot Press
PO Box 480, Guilford, Connecticut 06437-0888, United States of America

Distributed in Barbados by:
Best of Barbados Limited, Welches, St. Thomas, Barbados, West Indies. Tel: (246) 421-6900; Fax: (246) 421-6393; E-mail: bob@caribsurf.com

ISBN 0-7627-0596-5
A catalogue record for this book is available from the British Library
Library of congress Cataloging-in-Publication data is available

Copyright © Indigo Books Limited 2000
All photographs by: Duncan Willetts and Debbie Gaiger, except for Chris Huxley (page 1, bottom right; 47); and Mike Seale who supplied all the underwater photographs

Designed by: RB Graphics, "Rickettswood", Norwood Hill, Horley, Surrey RH6 0ET United Kingdom
Editors: Barbara Balletto and Debbie Gaiger
Proof-reading: Liz Sutherland

Printed and bound in China by Jade Productions

indigo guide to barbados

The Globe Pequot Press

Guilford, Connecticut

CADOGAN
island guides

London, England

ents

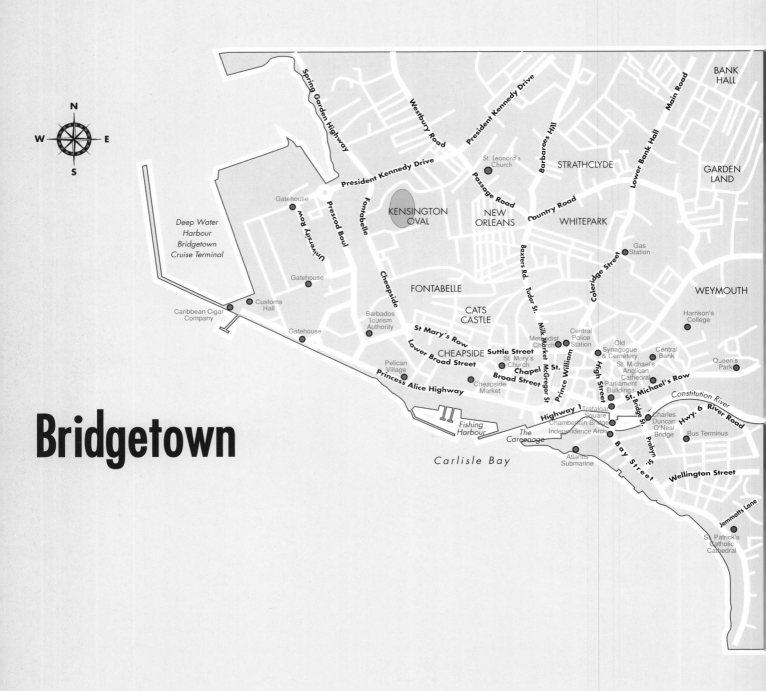

Bridgetown

N W E S

BANK HALL

GARDEN LAND

STRATHCLYDE

Spring Garden Highway

Westbury Road

President Kennedy Drive

President Kennedy Drive

Main Road

Lower Bank Hall

Barbarees Hill

Gatehouse

Prescod Boul

University Row

Fontabelle

St. Leonard's Church

Passage Road

NEW ORLEANS

Country Road

WHITEPARK

KENSINGTON OVAL

Deep Water Harbour Bridgetown Cruise Terminal

Gatehouse

Cheapside

FONTABELLE

Baxters Rd.

Tudor St.

Coleridge Street

Gas Station

WEYMOUTH

Gatehouse

Barbados Tourism Authority

CATS CASTLE

Harrison's College

Caribbean Cigar Company

Customs Hall

St Mary's Row

Lower Broad Street

CHEAPSIDE

Suttle Street

St. Mary's Church

Methodist Church

McGregor St.

Central Police Station

Old Synagogue & Cemetery

St. Michael's Anglican Cathedral

Central Bank

Queen's Park

Gatehouse

Pelican Village

Chapel

Broad Street

Prince William

High Street

St. Michael's Row

Cheapside Market

Princess Alice Highway

Highway 1

Trafalgar Square

Parliament Buildings

St. Bridge St.

Constitution River

Hwy. 6 River Road

Fishing Harbour

Chamberlain Bridge

Independence Arch

The Careenage

Charles Duncan O'Neal Bridge

Bay Street

Probyn St.

Bus Terminus

Carlisle Bay

Atlantis Submarine

Wellington Street

Jemmotts Lane

St. Patrick's Catholic Cathedral

Barbados

North Point
Archers Bay
Animal Flower Cave
Stroud Bay

PARISH OF ST LUCY
St. Lucy's Parish Church
Cuckold Point

Maycock's Bay
Mount Gay Distillery
St. Nicholas Abbey
Paul's Point
Gay's Cove
Pico Teneriffe

Six Men's Bay
Barbados Wildlife Reserve
Cherry Tree Hill
Grenade Hall Forest and Signal Station
Morgan Lewis Beach

SPEIGHTSTOWN
St Andrew's Parish Church
Morgan Lewis Sugar Mill

PARISH OF ST PETER

Mullins Bay
Mullins

PARISH OF ST ANDREW
Barclays Park

Turner's Hall Woods
Chalky Mount Potteries

PARISH OF ST JAMES
Mount Hillaby
Flower Forest of Barbados
BATHSHEBA

St James Parish Church
Sir Frank Hutson Sugar Machinery Museum
PARISH OF ST JOSEPH
St Joseph's Parish Church
Andromeda Botanic Gardens

HOLETOWN
Welchman Hall Gully
Hackleton's Cliff

Sandy Lane Bay
PARISH OF ST THOMAS
Harrison's Cave
St John's Church
Conset Bay

Paynes Bay
Villa Nova
PARISH OF ST JOHN

University of the West Indies
Earthworks Studio
Codrington College and Gardens
Cummins Hole
Skeete's Bay
Culpepper Island

Batts Rock Bay
Francia Plantation House
Ragged Point
East Point Lighthouse

Tyrol Cot Heritage Village
PARISH OF ST MICHAEL
Gun Hill Signal Station
Kitridge Point

National Stadium
Drax Hall
Bushy Park Racing Circuit

Mount Gay Visitor's Centre
St. George's Parish Church
PARISH OF ST PHILIP
King George V Memorial Park Gardens
Bottom Bay
Cove Bay

Sherbourne Center
PARISH OF ST GEORGE
Sam Lord's Castle

Government House
Daphne's Sea Shell Studio

BRIDGETOWN
Errol Barrow Memorial Park Sports Complex
Beachy Head
Crane Beach
Crane Bay
Cobblers Rock
Foul Bay

Garrison Savannah
The Barbados Museum
PARISH OF CHRIST CHURCH

Needham's Point
Hastings

Accra Beach
Rockley Beach
Worthing
Graeme Hall Swamp
Christ Church Parish Church

ST LAWRENCE GAP
OISTINS
Grantley Adams International Airport

Silver Sands

South Point Lighthouse

East Coast Road

0 1 2 3 4 miles
0 1 2 3 4 5 6km

N W E S

essential lists

lively places to get uncorked ...

- The Red Rooster
- Bourbon Street
- Café Sol
- The Boatyard
- Mullin's Beach Bar
- Crocodile's Den
- After Dark
- Harbour Lights
- The Rusty Pelican
- The Ship Inn
- The Waterfront Café
- The Lone Star Bellini and Cocktail Bar

great buys ...

- Mount Gay Rum
- Fine art by the island's best artists
- Hand-painted clothing
- Tapes or CDs of local musicians
- Handbags or leather goods
- Colourful T-shirts by Ganzee
- Local pottery
- Hand-made crafts and jewellery
- Shell art
- Colourful batiks

lively places to eat ..

- Ragamuffins
- Angry Annie's
- The Shak-Shak
- Champers
- Bourbon Street
- The Waterfront Café
- Nico's
- Oistins Fish Fry
- Bellini's
- Bean 'n Bagel Café

great places to visit ...

- Andomeda Gardens
- Barbados Wildlife Reserve
- The Garrison and Barbados Museum
- St Nicholas Abbey
- The Flower Forest
- Sunbury Plantation House
- Francia Plantation House
- Harrison's Cave
- Mount Gay Rum Visitor's Centre
- Tyrol Cot Heritage Village
- Orchid World
- Codrington College
- Welchman Hall Gully

fabulous places to eat
if money's no object ...

- The Lone Star Restaurant
- The Cliff
- The Carambola Restaurant
- Olives
- La Maison
- Mango's by the Sea
- Pisces Restaurant
- The Cobbler's Cove Hotel
- The Bagatelle Restaurant

great beaches ...

- Gibbs Beach
- Crane Beach
- Foul Bay
- Accra Beach
- Morgan Lewis Beach
- Mullins Beach
- Brighton Beach
- Payne's Bay
- Sandy Beach
- Silver Sands Beach

great experiences ...

- A sunset cruise aboard the *Jolly Roger*
- A visit to *Tropical Spectacular* at the Plantation Restaurant
- An underwater voyage on the *Atlantis* submarine
- Learn to scuba dive or just snorkel on the island's pristene reefs.
- Participate in a Barbados National Trust Sunday hike
- Parasail above the beaches
- Visit the Friday night fish-fry at Oistins on the south coast
- Take a flight on Bajan Helicopters for a bird's-eye view of the island
- Swim with turtles on the west coast
- Experience one of the island's dazzling festivals

......th...

Left: Bird's eye view of the Atlantic pounding the north coast of Barbados. Centre: The white sands of the west coast. Above right: Smiling children enjoy the sunshine. Above: Golden sunset paints dramatic shadows over the sparkling waters of the Caribbean Sea. Opposite: Pottery by Juliana is sold in various craft centres around the island.

barbados experience

An old man leads a donkey laden with sugar cane through the fading evening light, past a small stone church that doubles as a hurricane shelter and on down to a hamlet below. Crickets and tree frogs begin their nightly song, swelling to crescendo that fills the inky darkness. A breeze ripples through the canefields, bringing with it the exquisite aromas of frangipani and jasmine.

On the other side of the island gleaming "maxi-taxis" weave through the rush hour traffic, horns blaring, reggae and rhythm thumping from within. Along the south coast road en route to the tourist apartments and hotels they pass neon-lit nightclubs, drive-through restaurants and satellite television bars.

Contrast is the essence of life in Barbados. Its diverse cultural heritage, coupled with its isolated location, has given the island and its people a unique identity, made up of many different strands.

Geography

Barbados sits at the southern end of the Caribbean chain, latitude 13° west longitude 59° north. One hundred miles (160 km) to the east are the islands of St. Lucia and St. Vincent; to the south some 200 miles (320 km) away is Trinidad, just a stone's throw from the South American mainland. The North American cities of Miami and New York are 1,600 and 2,000 miles (2,500 and 3,200 km) to the north-east respectively. A predominantly flat island, Barbados is 21 miles (34 km) long and 14 miles (22 km) across at it widest point, with a surface area of 166 square miles (430 sq. km).

Geology

Barbados sits above the junction of two of the earth's great tectonic plates. As one was forced up and over the other, the overlying sediment rose from the sea floor and emerged from the ocean, forming the island's base. Coral growth and the subsequent deposits of limestone (the coral polyp produces its own limestone exoskeleton) gave the island its coral cap, 300 feet (91 metres) thick in some places and estimated to be between 750,000 and one million years old. This cap has been completely eroded in places; evidence of the powerful forces that worked to shape the island can be seen in the contorted folding and twisting of the sedimentary strata below.

Particularly interesting examples of this can be seen in the Scotland District of St. Andrew.

Although flat compared to its volcanic neighbours, Barbados possesses a variety of different landscapes. The north shore of the island is lined with jagged coral cliffs, pounded by relentless breakers that send a fine mist drifting gently inland. The eastern parishes are generally steeply wooded, save for a narrow strip of coastal land with wide open windswept beaches and pounding waves. Dominating much of the eastern landscape is Hackleton's Cliff, formed by tidal erosion of the island's coral cap at a time when sea levels were much higher. At almost 1,000 feet (305 metres) above sea level, it offers breathtaking vistas of the surrounding countryside.

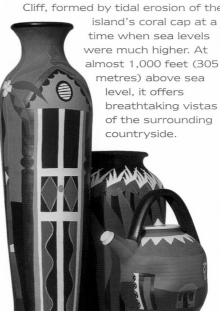

Much of the south coast is flat and comparatively arid, but because it faces the open Atlantic, it is cooled by the ever-present tradewinds. The west coast is home to most of the island's tourist-brochure beaches: long expanses of fine sand fringed with coconut trees and feathery casuarinas. Much of the island's lush interior is given over to agricultural production and is a patchwork of small tenant farms and sugar estates. Turner's Hall Wood, Foster Hall Wood and parts of Hackleton's Cliff are the only surviving examples of the dense tropical forest that originally covered Barbados.

Climate

The climate in Barbados has been described as the best in the Caribbean – and is still occasionally prescribed by doctors as a cure for some ailments! Winter temperatures range from 70 to 85°F (21 to 20°C), summer from 76 to 87°F (24 to 30°C). The lowest ever recorded temperature is 59°F (15°C) – the average being 80°F (26°C). The rainy season lasts officially for six months beginning June 1, and the island has an average annual rainfall of 60 inches (152 cm). September, October and November bear the brunt of the rainfall, with October being the wettest of all. Most rain falls as short heavy showers, but there are also protracted rainstorms that cause flash-floods: the heavy runoff quickly overwhelming culverts and storm drains, often causing extensive flooding. Although it is in the hurricane belt, Barbados is not considered a high-risk destination, as almost all hurricanes track north of the island.

Settlement, Slavery and Political Development

Barbados is believed to have been settled as early as 2,000 years ago by South American Indians, but little evidence remains of their early presence. The first documented settlement was by the Arawaks, a tribe of Amerindians from Venezuela, who arrived somewhere around 400 BC. They fished and farmed until AD 1200, when their population drastically declined, probably due to the arrival of the more aggressive Carib Indians. They are believed to have killed the Arawaks or forced them to flee, and lived on the island for a further 300 years.

Left: The dazzling white sands of Dover Beach in the south of the island. Centre: Colourful shutters decorate many chattel houses around Barbados. Opposite: Sugar was the mainstay of the island's economy in the seventeenth century.

When the English first set foot on Barbados in 1627 the island was uninhabited, the Caribs probably having been captured by the Spanish and Portuguese, who sent them to work as slaves in the mines and on plantations of the larger islands. Claiming the island in the name of King James, the English returned to settle some two years later, landing at Holetown on 17 February, 1627. This initial settlement was financed by Sir William Courteen, a wealthy London merchant who had obtained a deed to Barbados from the Crown. Tenant farmers originally grew crops such as tobacco and cotton, but neither fared particularly well and life was rigorous and hard for these early settlers.

Courteen lost his hold on Barbados some two years later when King Charles I granted proprietary rights to the Earl of Carlisle in what came to be known as "The Great Barbados Robbery". It was not until 1663 that this proprietary system was abolished and the island came under the direct rule of the British Crown. In-fighting between the Courteen and Carlisle factions worsened the island's already fragile economy, and a drought and subsequent drop in food production led the mid-1600s to be christened "The Starving Time". Although supporters of both factions existed on the island, they chose to put their differences aside and for the most part lived in harmony.

A steady trickle of settlers continued to arrive in Barbados, including many of the poorer classes from Europe, who, unable to afford to buy land, would agree to work as indentured servants for a number of years, after which they would be granted a parcel of land or a cash sum. Although a few African slaves did arrive with the first party of settlers, it was these indentured servants who made up the bulk of the

labour force. By the 1640s the Civil War in England was under way and a new influx of settlers began to arrive. Barbados had by now acquired a reputation of being a wild frontier, settled by a mixture of political escapees, fortune hunters, gamblers, vagrants and crooks. Several early historical accounts make reference to the seemingly uncivilized nature of the island.

It was not until the introduction of sugar cane in 1637 and the subsequent growth of the sugar industry that the island's fortunes began to change. The crop was introduced by a Dutchman, Pieter Blower, who had learned the practices of cane cultivation in Brazil. Initially planted to produce rum, by the early 1640s it was being planted

for sugar, a much more lucrative crop – and one which, more than anything else, was to shape the future of the island. The Dutch already dominated trading in the Caribbean and offered a ready market for sugar, as well as expertise and advice on sugar processing and the finances needed to set up and maintain sugar plantations.

The Dutch also introduced the planters to the West African slave trade. Vast tracts of land were cleared for cane cultivation and thousands of West African slaves were imported to work on the plantations. Between 1640 and 1807 some 490,000 slaves were brought to Barbados, many of whom were resold and sent to other territories. By the early 1500s slaves outnumbered whites two to one, and by 1684 there were 60,000 slaves, outnumbering whites four to one. The number of white indentured servants had dropped to around 2,000; much less than in earlier years.

With the vast profits realised by sugar production, the planters became immensely rich and enjoyed a period of great prosperity in the mid-17th century, the island becoming one of Britain's wealthiest colonies. Life for the slave, however, was far from good. Housed in bare-floored huts, they worked twelve hours a day, six days a week, surviving on meagre food rations with minimal clothing. About seventy-five per cent worked in the fields; the remainder in and around the plantation house, yard or sugar factories. Cooks, child-minders, butlers and gardeners were retained by most households and a variety of trades were taught to others to fill the skilled positions needed to keep the plantation system running. They were generally treated better than the field workers, but were nonetheless still slaves.

Discontent had been voiced as early as 1634 when the first slave rebellion occurred. Both that, and another attempt in 1639, failed as the number of slaves was too small. Since they came from many different countries in Africa there were few customs – not even a common language – that bound them together. The planters discouraged any form of African rituals and beliefs and tried to prevent any form of unity amongst slaves. Many believed the planters possessed some kind

Left: Jill Walker, one of the island's most renowned artists, has produced many lively paintings of island life. Opposite: A statue of the slave Bussa stands on the ABC Highway.

of magical powers and that their churches were used to perform witchcraft, placing spells and curses on the slave population. Slaves were issued with passes in order to restrict their free movement, and there were severe penalties for those involved in any sort of rebellion. The British Parliament granted the planters the right to put down uprisings by whatever means necessary, and a strong militia was formed. The first organised uprising in 1675 failed because a slave informed on the perpetrators. Nevertheless, seventeen of them were executed. There were other unsuccessful attempts at rebellion in the latter part of the 17th century, many of them thwarted at the last minute by informers loyal to their masters. It was not only black slaves who tried to revolt: a plot by a group of white servants was discovered and foiled; this time eighteen were put to death.

Living conditions improved for many slaves during the 18th century, especially for those born in Barbados, who were favoured over newly arriving Africans. A lot of the tension of earlier years ebbed away and Barbadian planters acquired a reputation of

giving more concessions to their slaves than those in other islands. Effectively the property of the planter, a slave could be freed only by his or her owner. This might be willed in the event of a planter's death, could occur when the slave reached a certain age, or merely come about as an act of compassion.

Slavery was officially abolished by the British Parliament in 1807, although it was to be many years until the practice actually ceased in Barbados. Concerned that the colony might have ignored the

decree, a Bill was passed in the British Parliament in 1815 requiring all slaves to be registered. The slave population became aware of the passing of the Bill, but believed it to mean *emancipation,* and not *registration.* Angered by the planters' apparent disregard of the Bill, they took matters into their own hands the following year. On the night of Easter Sunday 1816, cane fields in St. Philip were set ablaze and the insurrection quickly spread to neighbouring parishes. Plantation houses were sacked and burnt and twenty per cent of the sugar crop was destroyed. The planters' response was swift and unmerciful – 176 blacks were killed and a further 214 executed after trial. As a consequence the island was allowed to pass its own Slave Registry Bill, further strengthening the hand of the planters, but much more importantly the uprising succeeded in sowing firmly the seeds of emancipation. The slave Bussa, whose statue stands on the ABC Highway, is widely acknowledged as being the leader of the 1816 uprising.

International pressure led to the passing of the Emancipation Act in 1833, but it was not until

1 August, 1838 that the slaves were finally freed. With a few wealthy planters owning most of the land, the newly emancipated population had few places to go. The Masters and Servants Act of 1840 tied labourers to their former plantations and was a way of ensuring the labour force necessary to maintain the plantations. True emancipation was still a long way away.

The island's first political body was the House of Assembly, established in 1639 by Governor Henry Hawley, himself appointed by the Earl of Carlisle. For over 200 years the House was solely the domain of the white "plantocracy", but history was made in 1843 when Samuel Jackman Prescod, son of a black mother and white father, became the first non-white to become a member of Parliament. Until his death in 1871 he championed the causes of the masses, pressing for reform and helping to found the Liberal Party, which he led for more than twenty years.

Top: The Animal Flower Cave at the barren north of the island was created by the battering of the Atlantic waves over thousands of years. Centre: Colourful traditional buildings make up the Chattel Village in Holetown. Bottom: Photograph of the Pottery Market circa 1940. Opposite: Much of the island's interior is made up of small farms.

In 1876 the British government proposed that Barbados be linked with other regional territories in a loosely-knit confederation of the British West Indies. The plan was violently opposed by the ruling elite of Barbados, who had been effectively self-governing since the island was first settled. They were afraid of losing control of their cheap labour force, who would then be free to emigrate in search of better working conditions, or might gain a stronger political foothold under the new system of government. The Governor, Pope Hennessy, favoured the move towards becoming a Crown Colony and did his best to persuade the British Parliament to agree to it. Their refusal to consider such a move led to the outbreak of rioting and ultimately to the departure of Pope Hennessey to a posting in Hong Kong.

Democratic reform was slow – less than one per cent of the population at this time was entitled to vote – and by the end of the 19th century the white plantocracy still had a firm grip on the island's economy. A fall in sugar prices and discontent among the working classes led to the emigration of thousands of labourers – 20,000 alone went to work on the Panama Canal between 1850 and 1914. Many returned with money, and for the first time were able to buy their own land. Many of the planters were now heavily in debt and only too glad to shed some of the burden. Barbados found new markets for its sugar and, with the introduction of fertilizers and new cane species, produced record yields in the 1890s that helped offset the low price of sugar and kept the industry afloat.

However, conditions for the masses were still poor and several natural disasters conspired to make them even worse. Eighty people were killed and 18,000 houses destroyed by a hurricane in 1898; a smallpox epidemic struck in 1902, followed six years later by an outbreak of yellow fever. Very few could afford to send their children to school, and the government did little to alleviate the poverty that afflicted the majority of the population. Employment opportunities abroad were restricted and the completion of the Panama Canal in 1914 brought to a close what had been a profitable avenue of escape for many. With nowhere to go, most worked as tenant farmers on plantation land. The great depression of the 1930s

dealt a further blow to the economy and the seeds of discontent were firmly sown.

A new political force had emerged in the 1920s in the form of Dr Charles Duncan O'Neale. O'Neale founded the Democratic League in 1924, the first political party to represent the masses. Several candidates were elected to the House of Assembly, including O'Neale himself in 1932. One year later he founded the Workingmen's Association, the forerunner of the modern Trade Union movement. At the same time black consciousness and unity was being preached by followers of Marcus Garvey, a Jamaican. A powerful voice in the fight against the oppression of blacks, he wanted – among other things – to see an eventual return to Africa. More importantly he gave blacks a leader with whom they could identify.

Enter now a Trinidadian, Clement Payne, born of Barbadian parents. Payne was a fervent activist and public speaker who pushed hard for the formation of trade unions at public meetings in Bridgetown. So worried were the authorities by Payne's activities that they deported him from Barbados on July 26, 1937. Protesting against his deportation, angry crowds

gathered in public meeting places across the island. As the numbers swelled their mood turned ugly, and violent rioting erupted. Spreading quickly throughout the island, it was three days before it could be brought under control. It was not so much the deportation of Payne that was the object of their wrath, but the continuing economic and social oppression under which they lived. Although a "parliamentary democracy", thirty per cent of the national income was controlled by two per cent of the population.

Above: One of the fine paintings on display at the Kirby Gallery. Centre: Delicate water lily in the Andromeda Gardens. Opposite: Brightly-coloured catamaran on the white sands of Dover Beach.

The following year saw the formation of the Barbados Progressive League – also known as the Barbados Labour Party (BLP) – headed by Grantley H. Adams (later to become Sir Grantley). The league advocated greater equality for all, redistribution of wealth and eventual government control of production. It pushed for better working conditions, resulting in the legislation of the Trade Unions Act of 1939. The following year five of its members were elected to Parliament and were able to effect further change. Bills relating to old-age pensions and a minimum wage were passed, but attempts to change the electoral system were consistently blocked by the Legislature.

Finally, in 1942, women were granted the right to vote and to be elected to the House of Assembly. Political wrangling between the more liberal members of the General Assembly and the white conservative Legislative Council continued throughout the 1940s and saw the Council's powers gradually eroded. By the General Election of 1951, all Barbadians had secured the right to vote, and property qualifications for admission to the House of Assembly had been removed. Under the leadership of Grantley Adams, further changes to the constitution followed including the introduction of a Cabinet system in 1958, with the head of government becoming the Premier of Barbados.

The General Election of 1961 saw Errol Walton Barrow and his Democratic Labour Party (DLP)

come to power. A leftist politician with close ties to the Barbados Workers Union (established in 1941), Barrow had founded the party a year earlier after splitting from the BLP. He immediately embarked on an programme that included educational reform, expansion of the tourism industry, and the implementation of a National Insurance scheme. A large Public Works department was created, providing jobs for the unemployed and facilitating much-needed improvements to the island's infrastructure.

Barbados finally became a Sovereign State within the British Commonwealth on 30 November, 1966. Elections a few weeks earlier had seen Barrow win another term, and he stayed in power for a further ten years. Notable events during this period included the introduction of the Barbados dollar as the island's official currency in 1973, the formation of the Barbados Defence Force in 1978, and the opening of the Grantley Adams International Airport in 1979.

In 1976 the political tide changed again and the BLP was returned to power. It was re-elected for a second five-year term under the leadership of Sir Grantley's son, Tom Adams. It was his administration that was responsible for sending Barbadian troops to assist in the US-led invasion of Grenada in 1983, a move that proved unpopular with both Britain and some of the island's closer neighbours. The decision to base the US-sponsored Regional Security System in Barbados was regarded by many as another step toward Barbados becoming a political pawn of the US.

Playing on these fears, and drawing attention to the current state of economic stagnation and high unemployment, Barrow's DLP was returned to power in 1986 – winning all but three of the twenty-seven seats. Barrow died of a heart attack the following year and his deputy, Erskine Sandiford, became the new Prime Minister. Despite unpopular economic policies and internal differences which led to the defection of some of his ministers, Sandiford was re-elected in 1991. His troubles continued, and in 1994 he narrowly lost a no-confidence

motion. Surprisingly he refused to step down – a move that was seen by many to be the cause of his party's defeat at the General Election in September that year. The see-saw continued and the BLP were returned to power under the leadership of the current Prime Minister, Owen Arthur.

Today's political structure is based upon the British Parliamentary system with the Queen as Head of State. She appoints a Governor General as her representative, who in turn appoints the elected Prime Minister. There is an elected House of Assembly, whose members represent the island's twenty seven constituencies. An appointed Senate consists of twelve members from the majority party, two from the opposition, and seven appointees representing religious, social and economic interests. A Privy Council appointed by the Governor General deals with the grievances of civil servants and hears appeals from

convicted criminals; for those on "death row" it is the very last avenue of appeal. General Elections are held every five years unless the government chooses to call an early election (it may do so at any time) or loses a vote of no-confidence.

Since the mid-1960s, foreign investment has been actively encouraged via tax incentives for offshore companies, and today data-processing, captive insurance and offshore banking now form a significant part of the island's economy. Sixty per cent of the land area is given over to agriculture, with cane fields accounting for about half of that. Sugar still plays its part in the

CAFÉ
SOL
MEXICAN
GRILL & MARGARITA BAR

islands foreign-exchange earnings, but tourism is by far the major contender, with the number of annual long-stay visitors approaching the 500,000 mark. New golf courses, luxury residential developments and major hotel refurbishments have created a construction boom in recent years, and the island's economic well-being looks set to continue.

Barbadians

Barbados is one of the most densely populated countries in the world, with a little over 260,000 inhabitants. Whites account for only seven per cent of the population; seventy per cent are directly descended from African slaves. A combination of the two accounts for a further twenty per cent and the remainder is a mix of immigrant groups from as far away as India, the Middle East and China. The descendents of the original Scottish, Irish, and Welsh indentured servants occupy their own niche in the population. Known as "red-legs" because of

Top left: Golden sunset over Mullins Bay. Top right: The Barbados Gallery of Art. Centre: Hibiscus grow prolifically around the island. Bottom right: Harrison's Cave is made up of interconnecting caverns and underground chambers. Bottom left: Barbados has a wide selection of excellent restaurants and bars.

their kilt-wearing ancestors' propensity to sunburn, until recently they tended to live in close-knit groups where intermarriage was common. Although some communities still exist, they are more and more being assimilated into mainstream society.

More than half the population live in the two southern parishes of Christ Church and St. Michael in what are effectively suburbs of Bridgetown. The rest are scattered within small communities throughout the island, some consisting of no more than a rum shop, a church and a few wooden chattel houses. Many such settlements have their origin in the plantation era when they would have been the site of workers' quarters on the larger sugar estates. There are few "towns" in the conventional sense of the word – the best exception being Speightstown in St. Peter, which has well-laid-out streets, a waterfront promenade and a stately stone-built parish church.

Barbados has a well-deserved reputation for being the most friendly and hospitable of all Caribbean islands. There is a strong sense of unity amongst the island's inhabitants: they are first and foremost "Bajans", regardless of colour or creed. A five-minute walk through Bridgetown will reveal dread-locks, turbans, yarmulkes and perhaps a street-corner preacher toting a megaphone and Bible.

A visit to one of the island's many rum shops is a must for a truly Bajan experience. Often the social centre of a small village, these local bars double as general stores and have no licensing hours – save for the fact that they cannot open on election day until voting has finished. Heated discussions on cricket, politics and topical news are fuelled by liberal quantities of rum.

Bajans do not discuss things quietly, at least not in a rum shop. Instead they are given to shouting loudly at each other while gesticulating emotionally. Such behaviour may at first appear alarming, but it is done in good faith with no malice intended. A West Indies cricket test match at the Kensington Oval and the annual Crop-Over celebrations provide good opportunities to see the more boisterous side of the Barbadian character in action.

Cricket, often referred to as the national religion, incites great passion and is never without controversy. Everything possible is used to make a noise, and musical instruments such as drums, trumpets, and cymbals routinely find their way into the ground. Conch shells, klaxons, and tin cans filled with stones add to the atmosphere, and everybody – but *everybody* – has an opinion to voice. It is a great experience and a far cry from tea and cakes on the village green.

The Crop-Over festivities, which mark the end of the sugar cane harvest, culminate in the wildly colourful Kadooment Day procession from the National Stadium down to the end of the Spring Garden Highway. Thousands of exuberant revelers, many wearing ornate costumes, follow trucks carrying live bands or huge stereos, while thousands of spectators line the route.

Top: Barbados is a fabulous holiday destination for families of all ages.
Centre: Many chattel houses are painted in dazzling colours. Below: Bajans are passionate about cricket – a sport which is often referred to as the national religion.

The Bajan flair for colour is not restricted to Crop-Over, however. Grey suits rub shoulders with traditional African dress, and the very latest in North American and European fashions are on daily display. Many buildings, especially the small wooden chattel houses, receive electrifying paint jobs that leave the senses reeling.

There is, of course, a quieter side to the Bajan character. Like many of the West Indian islands, the pace of life is slow and a laid-back attitude predominates. The further one goes into the countryside, the more noticeable this becomes. Young men growling through Bridgetown in the latest model Toyota are apt to be replaced by older folk on foot or bicycle. Occasionally you will see a donkey-cart, a once common but now almost extinct form of transportation. Pass a stranger on foot and they will always

acknowledge your presence with a nod of the head, a wave, or a spoken greeting. Bajans are quick to offer advice and assistance and have a great sense of humour. Above all they are an optimistic and positive people, even in the face of adversity.

Religion and Superstition

Most Barbadians are deeply religious; at last count the island had well over 100 different religious sects and more churches than days of the year. Religion is everywhere – and in typical Caribbean colour and style. Seventh Day Adventists baptise their congregation in the cobalt blue seas, large funeral processions bring traffic to a standstill on the island's narrow roads, and Sunday morning sunshine is made brighter by the brilliant dresses and sharp-tailored suits of church-going families.

Churches come in all shapes and sizes, from the stately stone-built Anglican churches with their stained-glass and vaulted roofs to simple wooden structures containing nothing more than a few wooden benches for their revivalist congregations. In addition to regular church services, religious activities include choral recitations, fund-

raising dinners and garden parties, flower festivals, visiting crusades and gospel concerts – to name but a few.

There is only one truly indigenous religion in Barbados: the Spiritualist Baptist Church founded in 1957 by Archbishop Granville Williams. Its members are known locally as "tie-heads" after the colourful cloth which they wrap around their heads. With strong African influences, their services are powerful and emotional, often with much singing, dancing and ritual. Every Saturday night they hold a three-hour vigil in Trafalgar Square in Bridgetown. Other celebrations include a candle-lit procession on New Year's Eve through the residential districts

Left: Many stunning costumes are worn during the Kadooment Day festivities.
Below: The synagogue in Bridgetown is one of the oldest in the Western Hemisphere.

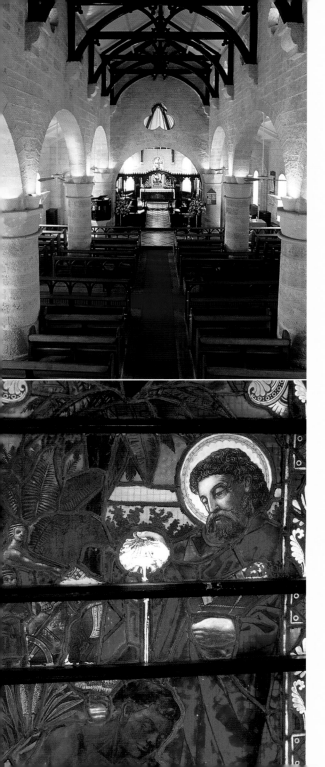

surrounding their cathedral in Christ Church, and a Palm Sunday procession that culminates in a baptism ceremony in the fishing village of Oistins. Their congregation numbers over 10,000 and they have built three churches on the island.

The only other West Indian religion practiced in Barbados is Rastafarianism. Introduced from Jamaica in 1975, it has its roots in Africa. Rastafarians believe the Ethiopian Ras Tafari – crowned in 1930 as Emperor Haile Selassie I – to be the "King of Kings, Lord of Lords and the Conquering Lion of the Tribe of Judah". A true Rastafarian wears his or her hair in dreadlocks, does not drink alcohol, and eats no meat – existing instead on a vegetarian diet. Many are involved in the field of arts and crafts – sculptors, painters, leather-workers and jewellers can be found in the Rastafarian Complex of Temple Yard in Bridgetown.

Religion has been an integral part of Barbadian life since the beginning – a chaplain was among the first party of settlers to arrive

Left: St. James's Parish Church in Holetown is one of the most attractive on the island. It has many fine examples of stained glass. Centre: One of oldest houses on the island in the historic Garrison area. Opposite: Cheerful Bajan youngster.

in 1629 and a church was one of the first buildings to be erected. Laws were passed making morning and evening prayer compulsory, with fines imposed for the neglect of family prayers, as well as for failure to attend church. Among the religions imported to Barbados in the early years, Judaism had a particularly important effect on the island's development, as it was Jewish settlers from Brazil who brought with them the knowledge and practices of sugar cane cultivation. The first synagogue was built for some 300 Jewish settlers in 1655, making it one of the oldest in the Western Hemisphere. It was destroyed by a hurricane in 1831 and, although quickly rebuilt, fell into a state of disrepair as many of island's Jewish settlers had by this time either emigrated or turned to Anglicanism. It was sold in 1929 and then repurchased by the modern though smaller Jewish community in 1983. Restored with the help of the National Trust, it witnessed its first Bar Mitzvah in April 1993.

Although the slave population was denied Christianity (often against the express wishes of the church) by the primarily Anglican "plantocracy", there were other

denominations who actively encouraged their membership. Quakers, Moravians, and Methodists all tried to convert the slaves – albeit it with limited success. Although generally tolerated, these faiths sometimes met with open hostility from the establishment. Blacks were banned from attending Quaker meetings from 1765 to 1810, and as late as 1823 the Methodist Chapel in Bridgetown was torn down by an angry mob.

Dissatisfaction and and dissent within the Anglican Church both in England and abroad led to the formation of "rival" religious factions. These groups divided further and new sects were formed, such as the Wesleyan Holiness and the African Episcopal Church.

Despite its earlier attitude toward the slave population, many slaves turned to the Anglican Church after Emancipation drawn perhaps by the respect and social mobility associated with it, and by promises of salvation. Others joined revivalist sects imported from the southern USA, where the fervour of their preachers and emotional involvement of the congregation provided a much livelier spiritual experience. The Roman Catholic Church finally gained acceptance the year after Emancipation when an Irish Battalion stationed in Barbados – the Connaught Rangers – requested a Catholic chaplain. Within two years the first Catholic church, St. Patrick's, was consecrated and later upgraded to a cathedral in 1970. Today there are six Catholic churches and over 10,000 communicants.

The Anglican Church remained the state church until its dis-establishment in 1969, and throughout the 19th century built many chapels, schools and churches across the island. It is still the most popular religion, accounting for about one-third of all church goers.

Many stories and superstitions of a religious nature abound in Barbados, among them several relating to the erratic behavior of lead and copper coffins inside sealed vaults. Of these, the most famous is that of the Chase family vault in Christ Church. On three occasions it was opened for burials and on each it was found that the coffins inside had moved from their original resting place. The Governor of Barbados decided to investigate the mystery for himself and duly attended the next burial, which took place in July 1819. Once more the coffins had moved. They were re-arranged to their rightful places, the floor sprinkled with sand and the door cemented shut. The Governor's seal was then applied in several places. Seven months later, in

the presence of thousands of onlookers, the tomb, with all its seals intact, was opened. The sanded floor showed no footprints, yet the coffins had moved: a heavy lead coffin now lay against the door of the vault, and several others were strewn about the interior. All the coffins were subsequently removed, and buried separately.

From the African heritage come stories of duppies, hags, and *obeah*. Some Barbadians, still speak of duppies, or spirits of the dead. These spirits take various forms and are said to roam the earth at night, returning to their favourite "haunts". Although many people adamantly deny the practice still goes on, believers and practitioners do exist. Various methods are used to discourage duppies from entering a house: hanging herbs at windows and doorways, leaving shoes at the door, or scattering sand around the house. Gifts of liquor are appreciated, and it is still a tradition to sprinkle a few

Top left: Ragamuffins is a lively bar and restaurant in Holetown. Top right: The inviting pool at the King's Beach Hotel. Bottom right: Artistically placed mirror on the beach at the Lone Star Restaurant. Centre: Lone catamaran takes to the water. Bottom: Scenic view across the immaculately-landscaped Flower Forest.

drops from a new rum bottle on the ground "for the spirits".

Many Barbadians believe that a dead person will "dream" you a few nights before he dies and, in so doing, convey an important message to you. Islanders hold vigils or wakes, called "nine-nights", to ensure a soul's safe passage to the other world. There are ceremonies in which the living talk to the dead for the purpose of "closure", inviting the dead to rectify unhappy situations they might have caused while still alive.

The most notorious of Barbados' folk beliefs is the system of *obeah*, a form of voodoo or witchcraft. The practice is believed to stem from a West African religion called *obi*. The British did their best to crush *obeah* from the beginning, forcing the practice underground. Today, it remains on the Statute Books of Barbados as a felony. Many claim that it no longer exists, while most will agree that its power is limited to those who believe in it.

Obeah potions are said to invest one with the power to succeed in one's endeavours and give control over others. Men have been tricked into marriage after unwittingly consuming the "come-

to-me sauce", which makes its victim irresistibly attracted to the woman who slipped it into his food. Wives are also known to have given their husbands "stay-at-home sauce" to curtail extra-marital philandering!

Although many people adamantly deny the practice still goes on, believers and practitioners do exist. The *Barbados Advocate* ran an interview in 1989 with a self-confessed "Doctor of African Science" who had been practicing for over sixty years. Using herbs and chemicals, he claimed – among other things – to be able to guarantee marriages and exorcise spirits. His clients were from all walks of life including prominent lawyers, doctors, and politicians.

Stories concerning *obeah* still surface. In 1989 residents of Thornbury Hill in Christ Church were reportedly besieged by a "Bacoo", a figure of miniature proportions and firmly entrenched in Barbadian mythology. Houses in the area were showered with sand and seaweed, although the nearest beach is miles away. Windows were broken by stones flying in slow motion, and a pot of rice inexplicably turned to a pot of rocks; these phenomena are also common in Barbadian folklore.

Fishermen

The unofficial emblem of Barbados is the flying fish: its likeness decorates hundreds of souvenir items and the island is often referred to as the "Land of the Flying Fish". It doesn't really *fly* – but instead uses its wing-like fins to glide for great distances over the water as it tries to elude its predators. Caught in vast numbers between October and July, it is a delicacy strangely shunned by many of Barbados' neighbours, who consider this small fish too much trouble to prepare. Flying fish accounts for seventy per cent of the island's total catch each year, with dolphin (not the *Flipper* variety, but a pelagic fish known elsewhere as mahi mahi or dorado) accounting for a further twenty-five per cent. The island has two major fishing centres – one is the fisheries

Above: Fishing boats are built locally and are usually brightly painted. Centre: Hand-painted ceramic tile. Opposite: Many fishermen set fish pots – hand made traps of wood and chicken wire.

complex in Bridgetown and the other the small fishing village of Oistins in the southern parish of Christ Church.

Most fishing boats are built locally from hardwoods and are referred to as launches. Powered by a single diesel engine, these brightly painted vessels can often be seen on beaches and roadsides as they undergo repairs and re-fitting during the off-season. The bright colours – although typical of the Caribbean – serve another purpose: they make the vessel more visible at sea. Each carries its registration number painted in large letters on the cabin roof for easy identification from the air.

The fisherman's day starts early; most are on the water by four in the morning. Heading offshore up to a distance of 15 miles (24 km), the launches employ a variety of both modern and traditional techniques to locate and attract fish. Depth sounders – also known as "fishfinders" – give an electronic picture of the waters below the boat and indicate the

presence of schooling fish. VHF radio keeps boats in touch with each other so that the location and nature of any discoveries can be shared by all.

Flying fish are caught in gill nets laid out manually behind the boat. They are attracted to the net by such devices as "screelers"; palm fronds towed behind the boat that provide shelter from the sun. Wicker chum baskets are trailed from the side of the boat, acting as bait for both flying fish and larger pelagic species. Long lines are also often employed which have many hooks along as much as a mile of heavy monofilament. The hooks are often baited with live flying fish and are designed to catch dolphin, tuna, and kingfish, among others. Bigger gamefish – such as blue and white marlin are not uncommon in the waters around Barbados.

Nets are pulled in by hand every so often, the catch removed, and the net reset. Bobbing around in the open ocean in a small boat is not for the fainthearted, with temperatures over 80°F (26°C) and the sea spray coating the skin in a thin film of salt. The cabin provides some respite from the sun, but is often the most uncomfortable place to be, especially if your only companion is a malodorous diesel engine. Boats are usually in by mid-afternoon in time to deliver their catch to the fishmarket. More recently there has been an increase in the use of commercial long-liners who put to sea for a week or two equipped with hydraulically driven winches, many miles of line and hundreds – if not thousands – of hooks. The number of ice boats in the industry has risen too. These carry insulated holds in which fish can be kept frozen, allowing the boats to venture further afield and stay out over a period of days.

Seine netting occurs closer to shore and, although not nearly as prevalent as gill netting, is a common sight. Operating from an open boat, fishermen lay a net out in a large circle and gradually pull it tight, trapping the fish inside. It is then hauled onto the boat, a laborious and time-consuming job that requires many pairs of hands.

Another familiar practice is cast netting, which takes place either from a small dinghy known locally as a "Moses", or from the shore. A circular net weighted around the edge is carried over the shoulder,

and tossed expertly over schools of small baitfish, opening flower-like and descending on its unwary prey. Baitfish are most often used live on handlines to catch larger bottom dwellers, such as snapper and grouper.

Spear fishing is popular too, with many fisherman choosing to make their own hardwood guns rather than purchasing expensive imported models. There are many species of reef fish in Barbados, with parrotfish, jacks and barracuda being among the most tasty and most sought after.

Many fishermen set fish pots – hand-made traps of wood and chicken wire. The fish is enticed into the pot by a bait and, once in, has great difficulty finding its way back out. These are laid on the sea floor and checked every couple of days.

Fish, a staple diet in Barbados, can be bought fresh from a number of markets. The bigger ones – such as those in Oistins and Bridgetown – are purpose-built, others consist of no more than a few wooden tables and a set of scales located on the side of the road. Fishing is big business in Barbados, providing a livelihood for many and a healthy, delicious source of nutrition for countless more.

a sightseeing

Despite its relatively small size – a mere 144 square miles (370 sq. km) – Barbados has much to offer and can sustain both the intrepid explorer and laid-back sun-worshipper for weeks on end. There are endless organised tours and attractions, plus miles of empty beaches, open countryside and forested hills to explore. Whether it be world-class golf at the Royal Westmoreland or a Banks beer in a village rum-shop, there is something to suit everyone.

Getting around the island is easy. There is an extensive public transport system and it is rare to have to wait long for a bus. Services to the countryside are less frequent and it is well worth checking the schedules if you are planning to travel to the more outlying districts. A 'bypass' bus is often your best bet, as they travel directly between two points (such as Speightstown and Oistins) – which means you do not need to change buses *en route*. Government buses are blue, and the privately owned mini-buses are yellow. The fare is the same and is fixed for any single journey, whether it be half a mile or twenty. In addition to this there are 'route taxis' (also known as 'ZR Vans'), white with

pectacular

a purple stripe, that follow pre-determined routes. In general the smaller the bus the faster it goes – so be warned! There is no shortage of taxis either. The set rates between different locations are displayed at the cruise-ship terminal, at the airport, and at most hotel lobbies. If you are out in the countryside, be sure you establish in advance what currency your fare is quoted in.

There are many tour operators that offer sightseeing trips to a variety of locations. A lot of the activities described below are available in special packages – for example, Bajan Helicopters and Tiami Cruises offer a 'Sail and Soar' package.

Bicycles, motorbikes, cars and vans are available for hire from one of the island's many rental agencies. A valid driver's license is required and you will need to obtain a visitors' driving permit. In the unlikely event that your agency does not provide you with one, they are available from any police station and are valid for one year. Drive on the left-hand side of the road and exercise caution. Be prepared for potholes, schoolchildren, chickens, sheep and more. Pay particular attention to the open storm-drains that edge many of the island's roads.

Gas stations can be found throughout Barbados, but it is still a good idea to fill up at 'home' if you are planning on exploring the more remote parts of the island.

Survival kit

Essential 'survival' items include sun-screen and insect repellent. The sun's strength is often underestimated, especially if you are in a windy location such as an east coast beach or on a sailboat. A factor five or seven just will not cut it; fifteen is more appropriate for those already used to the strong sun and thirty for children and newcomers.

Barbadians have a well-deserved reputation for being hospitable, friendly and helpful, and are proud of their country and its tourism industry. Never hesitate to ask for advice and directions from strangers; they will be more than happy to assist. Things move slowly here, which is part of the charm of the place. The country operates on 'Bajan Time', not world time, so five minutes here is not the same five minutes one is used to in Europe or North America. Leave your hang-ups behind, let yourself go and chill out. You cannot beat this system, so join and enjoy it.

Exercise the same caution as you would anywhere in the world. The island may be a tropical paradise, but time has not passed it by. You may be pestered by beach vendors or self-appointed 'guides'. In both cases, the best way of dealing with them is a firm but polite 'no thank you'. Do not leave your valuables on view on the beach or in the car, and ensure your hotel room, apartment or villa is properly secured at night. If you are going to take a moonlight walk on the beach, do it in the company of some friends and avoid walking along deserted stretches of beach late at night.

If you follow these few suggestions, along with the more detailed advice in the Nitty Gritty section (page 144) your stay on the island will be a truly memorable, trouble-free trip-of-a-lifetime.

Opposite: The Andromeda Botanic Gardens is spread over a hillside on the east coast. Right: Peacocks meander through the lush mahogany woods that make up the Barbados Wildlife Reserve.

Bridgetown

The city of Bridgetown is one of much character and charm, containing a fascinating mix of architecture that ranges from traditional wooden chattel houses to the eleven-storey edifice of the Central Bank. There is plenty to see, and a leisurely walk through the city is a good way to spend some time.

A word of warning, however: as it gets quite hot here during the day, take care not to make your walk too long without stopping. The route described below covers most of the interesting points in the city and can be covered in forty-five minutes to one hour.

Broad Street is the city's main thoroughfare and shopping

street, and is lined with department stores, international retailers, cafés, banks, and more. Start your tour at the northern end in front of the imposing **Mutual Life Building** which was built in 1895.

At the southern end are the neo-Gothic **Parliament Buildings** which hold the island's two houses of parliament, the assembly and the senate. It was established in 1639 and is one of the oldest in the world. Visitors are welcome to watch from the public gallery when parliament is in session. In the debating chamber there is a series of stained glass windows which depict British sovereigns since James I. **Trafalgar Square** – complete with its own statue of **Lord Nelson** is on the north side of the **Chamberlain Bridge**, an old swingbridge that at one time let schooners pass into the inner basin. Here a vessel would be laid on its side and the hull cleaned, caulked, and painted, a procedure known as 'careening'.

Once across the bridge, drop down to the waterfront and walk along the length of the **Careenage.** The buildings on both sides were built as bonded warehouses and ships' chandlers and are among the city's oldest. They now house restaurants, bars, and boutiques, and deep-sea fishing boats and pleasure yachts abound. Turn left in front of Coral Isle Divers and walk back toward DaCosta Mannings, which sits at the north end of Bay Street. Bay Street contains some fine examples of traditional 'shop-houses', with the ground floor shop built of stone and the living quarters above of wood. Turn left and walk back toward the city across the **Charles Duncan O'Neale Bridge** which commemorates the man who founded the island's first political party. Bay Street continues south through the old red light district, along the shore of Carlisle Bay and up to the Garrison. Turn right at the traffic lights next to Julie's Supermarket and walk the short distance up to red-roofed **St. Michael's Anglican**

Cathedral. The present building dates from 1786 and incorporates some fine carvings, sculptures and colourful stained glass. Many of the island's prominent luminaries are buried in the churchyard, including Sir Grantley Adams. Leave the cathedral and walk along Roebuck Street to James Street on your right. This narrow road is fronted by old buildings, including the city's oldest – located at the corner of James and Lucas streets. Now occupied by law chambers, the building features classic Dutch gables characteristic of late 17th century architecture. The **Central Police Station**, **Law Courts**, **Public Library**, and **Synagogue** all border the car park at the end of James Street. Cross Tudor Street and continue

down Suttle Street to **St. Mary's Church**, which sits on the island's oldest piece of hallowed ground, consecrated in 1630. The church was built in 1827 and is a fine example of Georgian architecture. Pass the bus terminal opposite the church and walk past Courts department store and the **Rastafarian Market** of Temple Yard onto Hincks Street. A short walk from here leads back to the Mutual Building on Lower Broad Street.

Left: Bird's-eye view of the city of Bridgetown. Far left: The 19th-century Mutual Life Building is one of Bridgetown's most striking colonial buildings. Above: Independence Arch was erected in 1987 to commemmorate twenty-one years of Barbadian independence. Centre: A miniature bronze statue of Horatio Nelson stands in Trafalgar Square.

Barbados Wildlife Reserve

Located in St. Peter, near the top of Farley Hill and the border of St. Andrew.

Telephone: 422-2286

Fax: 422-8946

Hours: Open daily, 10am–5pm

Entrance fee: Reasonable, with reduced rates for children.

Facilities: Refreshments are available from the hut next to the information booth.

Opening its doors in 1985, the Barbados Wildlife Reserve is administered by the Barbados Primate Research Centre, which was established in 1979 to study the indigenous green monkey (*cercopithecus sabaeus*). In addition to the large, free-roaming monkey population, the reserve houses many other animals, including the largest collection of West Indian tortoises in the world. They can be found meandering along the stone pathways. During the mating season, they can be heard from one end of the reserve to the other. The reserve is heavily wooded with towering mahogany trees and contains such creatures as the reclusive brocket deer, agouti, and raccoons. Reptiles include caimans, terrapins, iguanas and a 10-foot (3-metre) python – the only animal on the reserve that is caged. The iguanas are an endangered species originally from Cuba and are bred in the reserve. A walk-through aviary houses a variety of birds, including the macaw and the colourful St. Vincent parrot. Two lilly ponds are home to pelicans, flamingos and otters. An interpretation centre provides information on the birds and animals of the reserve, as well as some background on the Primate Research Centre.

Top: Green monkeys first came to Barbados around 1650. Centre: The shy clawless otter spends many hours hiding in the undergrowth. Bottom: The reserve is home to a large collection of West Indian Tortoises. Below: Strikingly-coloured flamingos are found in the reserve.

Andromeda Botanic Gardens

Situated on a steep hill overlooking the small fishing village of Tent Bay just to the south of Bathsheba on the St. Joseph coast.

Telephone: 433-9261 or 433-9384

Hours: daily from 9am until 5pm

Entrance fee: Reasonable, with reduced rates for children.

Facilities: There is a 'Best of Barbados' gift shop and a small café at the entrance.

Willed to the Barbados National Trust in 1988, Andromeda Gardens has one of the finest collections of tropical plants anywhere in the Caribbean. It was the former home of the late Iris Bannochie, an avid horticulturist and author of several books on Caribbean flora. She started the garden in the early 1950s and travelled extensively, collecting plant specimens from many corners of the world that today can be found throughout the 8-acre (3-hectare) site. A small stream flows through the property and feeds two ponds, which are adorned with a covering of both day- and night-blooming lilies. Giant arrow arum grows in the lower pond, and the aquatic thalia produces a pair of mirror-image flowers that grow side by side.

Several huge coral boulders support interesting collections of mosses, lichens, liverworts, ferns, cacti, and succulents and were the first parts of the garden to be planted. Of particular note among these rock-dwellers are the scarlet-coloured flame violet, two indigenous species of anthurium, a night-blooming cactus, and the breadfruit and maidenhair ferns. The latter is a relative of the endemic Farleyense fern first discovered in the 19th century at Farley Hill in St. Peter. There are over seventy-five different types of heliconia and an extensive collection of palms – including the sealing wax palm with its bright red stalks and stems. There is also a magnificent example of the traveller's palm, and a tailpot palm which, like the century plant, flowers only once in its lifetime and then dies.

There is an large collection of vanda orchids and many eye-catching stand-alones, like the Easter lily tree with its huge, trumpet-shaped flowers. In all, there are some 700 plant species at Andromeda. With the assistance of a map, take a self-guided stroll over a meandering network of paths; the majority of the plants are labelled. Look for the small garden just outside the entrance, which is filled with brilliant hibiscus of every colour, shape, and size.

Left: The hibiscus garden features many many shades of this delicate flower. Above: Dazzling flamboyant tree.

Barbados Museum

The Barbados Museum and Historical Society sits at the edge of St. Anne's Garrison just to the south of Bridgetown.

Telephone: 427-0201 or
436-1956

Fax: 429-5946

Hours: Monday to Saturday from 9am–5pm; Sundays from 2–6pm. (Library open Monday to Friday from 9am–1pm.)

Entrance fee: Reasonable, with reduced rates for children.

Facilities: There is a gift shop at the entrance and a café in the courtyard. All of the major galleries are easily accessible to wheelchair users.

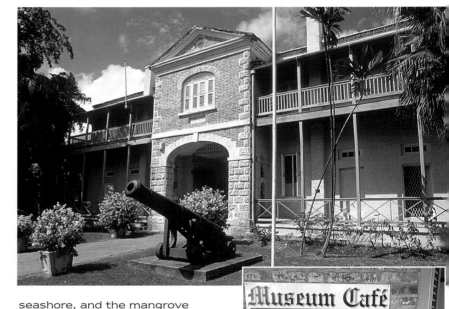

The Barbados Museum and Historical Society is housed in the Garrison's old military prison and offers a great introduction to the island through a number of well designed galleries.

As you pass through the reception area, you will come to the **Harewood Gallery,** which deals with natural history. Several lovely exhibits detail different ecosystems found on the island, including the coral reef, the seashore, and the mangrove swamp. Next is the **Jubilee Gallery,** which covers the history of Barbados in detail. The many exhibits here, include a large selection of period artefacts and photographs. Amerindians, bush medicine, religion, education, and law and order are all showcased, as are civil engineering, boat-building, the cotton industry, the plantation system, and much more. The next room is the **Aall Gallery,** which houses a comprehensive collection of maps dating back over a period of 350 years. Up a short flight of steps in the quadrangle is the **Warmington Gallery**, where a bedroom, nursery, and living room have been recreated in the style of a 19th-century plantation house.

The **Challenor Gallery** details the island's military history from the inception of the first Barbados Militia in 1640 to the present day. Among the many interesting artefacts are the remains of a German World War II torpedo that struck a merchant ship in Carlisle bay in 1942. Next to this is the **Cunard Gallery**, which contains a substantial collection of paintings and prints. The **Connell Gallery** has one room dedicated to African culture and another that is full of 17th-, 18th- and 19th-century glass, ceramics, and silverware.

The last permanent exhibit is the **Kidd Gallery** – a children's museum that gives a historical insight into the lives of the island's younger inhabitants. It contains a fine collection of model wooden boats and a large number of ornate hand-made dolls.

There is also a temporary gallery that hosts showings of work by top local artists. At the entrance to the museum is a gift shop that has an unusual collection of West Indian literature, postcards, prints, local crafts, and jewellery.

Upstairs is the **Museum Library**, which is open to the public. It holds over 5,000 books and has a comprehensive collection of old photographs, postcards, and newspaper clippings.

Opposite top: The museum's entrance is flanked by two cannons. Opposite: A welcoming smile outside the courtyard café. Left: The museum contains various exhibits on the Ameridians. Above: The Connell Gallery features traditional masks and instruments from around Africa.

Codrington College

Located just south of Bath in St. John's Parish, off the road from Martin's Bay.

Telephone: 423-1274

Fax: 423-1592

Hours: daily from 10am to 4pm

Entrance fee: Minimal.

Set in beautiful grounds with sweeping views of the Atlantic Ocean, Codrington Theological College in St. John is the oldest surviving seminary in the Western Hemisphere. The pioneer of the 19th-century theological college movement, it was founded by Christopher Codrington, a former Captain General of the Leeward Islands. On his death in 1710, he left his estates to the 'Society for the Propagation of the Gospel in Foreign Parts', with a wish to establish a community where scholars would study divinity and surgery ('doing good to men's souls, whilst they are taking care of their bodies') while living under monastic vows. It was a vision that pre-dated the Church of England's re-introduction of monastic life by 150 years.

Opened as a grammar school in 1745, it became a fully-fledged college in 1830. In 1875 it was affiliated with the University of Durham in England and became the only college in the West Indies where arts and theology could be studied to degree level. Since 1955 it has been affiliated with the University of the West Indies and today two-thirds of all West Indian clergy are educated at Codrington.

The college still functions as a seminary, as well as a conference centre, so access to some of the buildings is therefore restricted. However, the rest is open to visitors – as are the grounds.

The college buildings were completed in 1743 and feature an imposing triple-arched open portico modelled in the Italian Renaissance style. From the top of the lengthy driveway one can see straight through this portico and out to the open sea. The small chapel contains some beautifully-carved hardwood furnishings and has an interesting arrangement of dormer windows set high into a curved ceiling. The principal's lodge, adjacent to the college buildings, was built almost 100 years earlier and was the former home of Christopher Codrington himself. It was the original Great House of the sugar plantation and dispite damage by fire and hurricane, sections of the original building still remain. It has a unique entrance porch with stone arches and stone pillars that are built into each other.

A large lily pond dominates the gardens and a row of stately cabbage palms – some thought to

be more than a century old – line the college driveway. Legend has it that two of the original palms were planted by Prince Albert and Prince George during a visit in 1879. The one planted by Albert soon perished, followed shortly thereafter by the news from abroad that the Prince himself had died.

The five acres of woodland adjacent to the college feature a short, but beautiful, nature trail that includes many of the island's native trees. The names alone are intriguing and include the silk cotton tree, beefwood, garlic pear, macaw and galba.

Opposite: The buildings of Codrington College are arranged around an arched portico which opens onto landscaped gardens. Left: Elegant interior of the college. Above: The approach to the college is along a palm-lined avenue which ends beside an ornamental pool.

Flower Forest at Richmond Plantation

Located in St. Joseph, near the western edge of the Scotland District, a mile from Harrison's Cave, near Welchman Hall Gully.

Telephone: 433-8152

Fax: 433-8365

Hours: daily, 9am to 5pm

Entrance fee: Reasonable, with reduced rates for children.

Facilities: There is a Best of Barbados handicraft shop on the site, as well as a snack bar.

The 50-acre (20 hectare) Flower Forest sits some 850 feet (260 metres) above sea level and affords some spectacular views across the Scotland District and the east coast. The Richmond Plantation was originally a working sugar plantation that opened its doors to the public in 1983 after two years of restoration. The pathways through the forest are clearly laid out on a map that is given to visitors at the entrance. The paths are well maintained and the majority are accessible to wheelchair users.

There are hundreds of indigenous and imported trees in the forest, all labelled with their English and Latin names. Species include the African tulip, sandbox, bearded fig, powder puff , fishtail palm, breadfruit, hog plum, baobab, guava, mango, Jerusalem thorn and cabbage palm. A highlight of the forest is the Palm Walk which features different types of of shady palms.

Medicinal plants, poisonous plants, ferns, fruits, and decorative plants are all well represented and clearly labelled. Ginger lilies, anthuriums, 'Pride of Barbados', heliconias, bougainvillea, ixoras and vanda orchids are among some of the more colourful flora.

There are a number of garden benches, look-out points, and a small gazebo that is covered with flowering vines. A large open-air deck adjoins the main building and refreshments are available from the snack bar. There is a *Best of Barbados* gift shop and a mock-up of a sugar-boiling house that contains the original boiling vats used on the plantation. A ceramic mural depicts life at Richmond Plantation over the last 100 years.

Opposite top: Magnificent species of palm can be found in the Flower Forest. Centre: Scarlet poinsettia. Bottom: The forest offers spectacular views across the island.

Francia Plantation House

Situated on a wooded hillside just south of Gun Hill.

Telephone: 429-0474

Fax: 435-1491

Hours: Monday to Friday, 10am–4pm; closed holidays

Entrance fee: Minimal; includes a complimentary drink served on the veranda.

Francia Plantation House in St. George is a well-maintained private residence that has been open to the public since 1989. Still lived in by descendents of the original owner, it is one of the finest examples of plantation architecture and has been designated a house of architectural interest by the Barbados National Trust. It was built at the turn of the twentieth century by Frenchman Rene Mouraille, who moved here from Brazil after marrying a Barbadian. It contains an eclectic blend of architectural features not usually found in Bajan plantation houses. These include a sweeping flight of curved stone steps, a recessed entrance porch and balcony, and double 'Demerera' shutters.

The entrance hall is panelled and floored with *sucipira*, a Brazilian hardwood so dense that a nail will not pass through it. Maps from the 17th and 18th centuries hang on the walls, part of an extensive collection that date back to 1522. A Victorian love-seat in the centre of the room has three upholstered seats: one each for the lovers and the third for the chaperone!

Most of the furniture in the house was locally made between 1840 and 1860 of Barbadian mahogany; notable examples include the large dining room table (which can be extended to twice its size) and a beautiful three-piece suite in the drawing room. There are also imported antiques: a spectacular Venetian chandelier of Murano glass, a 300-piece silverware set from Tiffany, and an inlaid wooden games table for chess, backgammon, and cards that dates from 1720.

The house sits in spacious mature gardens with stone terraced lawns, fountains, and coral-stone balustrades and benches. A view through orchid-swathed trees looks out over the beautiful vale of St. George.

Above: Francia is a fine example of plantation architecture. Right: The mature gardens feature a charming ornamental pond.

Gun Hill Signal Station

Located in the middle of the island on the highland of St. George; inland from Highway 4 towards St. George's Church.

Telephone: 429-1358

Hours: Monday–Saturday, 10am–4pm with the exception of some public holidays

Entrance fee: Reasonable; reduced rates for children.

Facilities: A small gift shop,   a snack bar, and a veranda dining area.

Strategically placed in the centre of the island 700 feet (210 metres) above sea level is the Gun Hill Signal Station, one of a chain of six signal stations constructed in 1818 after the islands first and only slave revolt. It was opened to the public in 1982 after extensive restoration by the Barbados National Trust. Its primary purpose was to warn the military garrison in Bridgetown of the impending arrival of hostile ships. So successful was this system of defence that the island was never captured and remained in British hands right up until Independence in 1966.

The coral-stone and red-brick building consists of the signal tower, two bedrooms, and a small kitchen. All contain interesting period artefacts, including military paraphernalia, domestic implements, photographs, and illustrations. Two preserved cannons – one 9-pounder (4-kg) and one 24-pounder (11-kg) – sit outside on rare cast-iron garrison carriages. Six men lived in the station, with two in the signal tower at all times – they would signal using flags during the day and lanterns at night.

Overlooking the fertile St. George Valley, the signal station affords panoramic views: the airport, deepwater harbour, and city of Bridgetown are all clearly distinguishable on the seaward side, while the view inland traverses a patchwork of agricultural smallholdings and looks deep into the hilly parish of St. Thomas.

Down the road below the station is a large stone lion, carved by one Henry Wilkinson, a British officer stationed here in 1868. Part of the Latin inscription at its base bears testament to the prevailing sentiment of the time and translates to: 'It [the British Lion] shall rule from the rivers to the sea, and from the sea to the ends of the earth.'

Left: The white lion was carved from a single block of limestone in 1868. Above: Gun Hill was constructed on high ground so that stations could pass signals around the island in the event of attack.

Harrison's Cave

Situated close to Welchman Hall Gully in the parish of St. Thomas.

Telephone: 438-6640/1/3/4/5

Hours: daily from 9am–4pm; reservations recommended

Entrance fee: Reasonable, with reduced rates for children. Group discounts are available.

Facilities: A snack bar and gift shop are located inside the Visitor's Centre.

Harrison's Cave is one of the island's most interesting and unusual attractions. Although locals have been aware of its presence for generations, it was not until 1970 that the cave system was properly explored. A little over a decade later – after extensive work by the National Conservation Commission – it was opened to the public. There are about 3 miles (5 km) of interconnecting caverns, but only 1 mile (1.5 km) has been developed to date. In this subterranean labyrinth, there are waterfalls, lakes, streams, narrow passages, and cavernous underground chambers. Beautiful stalactites drip from the ceilings and huge stalagmites rise from the floor. It takes over 200 years for a stalactite to grow 1 inch (2.5 cm), and the age of the cave system is estimated at over 500,000 years.

Visitors don safety helmets and board an electric tram to begin a steep descent into the cave system. It begins with the Great Hall, the largest of the subterranean caverns. Divided into upper and lower levels, it measures some 250 by 100 feet (76 by 30 metres), with the floor at 120 feet (37 metres) below the surface and an almost perfectly domed roof towering overhead.

Subtle lighting emphasises particularly beautiful formations of stalactites and stalagmites such as 'The Altar' and 'The Village', and at one point during the tour all the lights are extinguished and the cave is plunged into a warm, damp, and absolute darkness. A lake marks the cave's natural entrance, and a small boat is moored here to evacuate passengers in case of emergency.

The deepest part of the system is at 160 feet (49 metres), where the 'Cascade Falls' plunge 40 feet (12 metres) into a deep blue-green pool.

Passengers are allowed to disembark and take photographs at intervals during the forty-five minute trip, and an informative guide explains the history and unique features of the cave.

There is also a short but interesting nature trail, which starts from the Visitor's Centre.

Helicopter Tours

Bajan Helicopters operate from the Barbados Heliport, in Bridgetown.

Telephone: 431-0069/0086

Entrance fee: Expensive, but the tours offer an exhilarating sightseeing experience; there simply is nothing quite like it.

Facilities: Handicapped passengers are welcome, and a babysitting service is provided at the heliport.

Using French-built Astar Jet helicopters – better known to Europeans as 'Squirrels' – Bajan Helicopters offer two trips: the 'Discover Barbados' and the 'Island Tour'. Each helicopter can accommodate five passengers plus the pilot, and operate at up to 16,000 feet (4,900 metres) with a maximum airspeed of 147 nautical miles.

The twenty-minute 'Discover Barbados' tour begins with a loop around Carlisle Bay and turns inland over the city of Bridgetown before dipping into St. George and over the old plantation house at Lion Castle in St. Thomas. It then continues over the Flower Forest and down to the picturesque village of Bathsheba on the east coast; then north along the beach and up and over Chalky Mount in St. Andrew, offering some spectacular views of the Scotland district. The flight turns inland at Cherry Tree Hill, passes St. Nicholas Abbey, over the ruins of the Great House in Farley Hill National Park to the town of Speightstown.

Above: The cruise ship terminal in Bridgetown. Right: Fabulous white sands on the West Coast.

Turning south, the flight runs the length of the west coast beaches, passes over the deep-water harbour and returns to base.

The 'Island Tour', which lasts about thirty minutes, takes off and heads immediately south over the flat expanse of Carlisle Bay, past Needham's Point and down the densely-populated south coast strip as far as the fishing village of Oistins and the adjacent South Point Lighthouse. Here the flight turns inland to skirt the airport and returns to the coast at Crane Beach. The route continues north over Sam Lord's Castle, up the St. Philip coastline to the lighthouse at Ragged Point, and then on toward Bathsheba – with a quick detour inland to view St. Johns Church and Codrington College on the way. The flight then heads right up the length of Morgan Lewis Beach to Pico Tenerife in St. Andrew, around the rugged north shoreline to Animal Flower Cave and North Point Lighthouse in St. Lucy. Next the helicopter travels south, past the Arawak

Cement Plant, over the marina at Port St. Charles, and on to Speightstown. From here the run back to the heliport is the same as the 'Discover Barbados' itinerary.

In addition to regular tours, helicopters are available for photographic and video shoots (two to three days notice is required),

tanker transfers, and aerial surveys. It also offers passenger transfers between Grantley Adams International Airport and the resort communities of Royal Westmoreland and Port St. Charles. Bajan Helicopters operate three aircraft and have recently purchased a larger twin-engine helicopter to facilitate charters between neighbouring islands.

Above: The dazzling sands contrast sharply with the azure waters of the Caribbean Sea at Miami Beach. Left: Bajan Helicopters.

Orchid World

The garden can be found in the parish of St. George between Gun Hill and St. John's Church on Highway 3B.

Telephone: 433-0306

Hours: daily from 9am to 5pm

Entrance Fee: Bds$13.80 for adults and half price for children

Facilities: The entire garden is wheelchair accessible. There is a Best of Barbados gift shop and a small snack bar in the reception area.

The stunning Orchid World is situated 841 feet (246 metres) above sea level in the high rainfall sector of Barbados. Here hundreds of dazzling orchids are showcased in a breakhtaking environment of natural caves, ponds, waterfalls and streams.

There is a shady grotto area of caves and coral boulders carpeted with maidenhair ferns and some of the climbing plants that grow wild in Barbados. On leaving the grotto, a path leads to the lower level of the gardens where many different species of orchid are

exhibited. They are grown on wire frames to stimulate growth and this area is ablaze with multi-coloured shades of this exotic delicate flower.

There are various houses which provide the correct conditions for growth, particularly the moist atmosphere they require to stimulate their growth. Rainwater is used for irrigation wherever possible and is provided by collecting water in a specially constructed 30,000 gallon tank beneath the deck of the main building. All the irrigation features of the complex are designed so that water can be recycled as much as possible.

There are fabulous examples of a variety of orchids, including Vanda, Ascocendas, Phalaenopsis, Cattleyas, Oncidiums, as well as *Miss Joaquim*, the national flower of Singapore. In the first house, the orchids tagged with bright green or orange labels are exquisitely fragrant.

A walk through the gardens leads to a magnificent view across sugar cane fields over several parishes around the island.

Left: Hundreds of fabulous orchids are on display in the spectacular Orchid World.

Mount Gay Rum Visitor's Centre

Located toward the Bridgetown end of the Spring Garden Highway in Exmouth Gap.

Telephone: 425-8757

Fax: 425-8770

Hours: Tours are conducted every half-hour between 9am–4pm, Monday–Friday.

Entrance fee: Reasonable; includes tasting.

Facilities: Veranda restaurant.

Mount Gay makes the oldest rum in the world; its distillery in St. Lucy having been in continuous production since 1703. Half a million gallons of rum are produced each year, including varieties such as Eclipse, Extra Old, Sugar Cane Brandy, Premium White, and Overproof.

Tours start with a video presentation inside an air-conditioned theatre that resembles the interior of a traditional Bajan rum shop. This twelve-minute clip touches on the geology and geography of Barbados, the introduction of sugar cane and subsequent growth of the sugar industry, the history of Mount Gay and the various processes involved in the production of rum. A lively and informative guide then takes visitors through the plant and explains each step in the production process. Fermentation and distillation, the first steps in rum production, take place at the St. Lucy distillery. This produces both single and double distillates, which are then shipped to the Spring Garden plant and set to age in charred oak barrels for between two and twelve years.

The warehouse holds over 4,000 barrels and as you walk between them you can smell the heady 'Angels Share' – the seven per cent that evaporates during the aging process and drips from the ceiling. You visit the cooperage where the barrels are made, and get a bird's-eye view of the bottling

plant, capable of producing 18,000 bottles a day. The thirty- to forty-minute tour concludes with a tasting session where the precise and proper way to taste a spirit is demonstrated. There is a well-stocked bar and veranda restaurant, and Mount Gay rum is available for sale. Souvenirs and clothing bearing the Mount Gay logo are also available.

Death in the Afternoon
A large measure of Mount Gay Overproof (151) rum, 4ozs (120 ml) of Mount Gay Rum Punch, 2ozs (60 ml) of orange juice and a dash of Angostura bitters.

Left: The storage area in the factory is crammed with barrels. Above: Chester mixes delicious cocktails in the bar at the Visitor's Centre where visitors are invited to sample various blends of Mount Gay Rum.

St. Nicholas Abbey is the oldest of the island's Great Houses, although it was never an abbey (an owner simply christened it as such). It is of particular architectural interest, and is one of only three Jacobean plantation houses left in all of the Americas.

Believed to have been built in the 1650s by Colonel Benjamin Berringer, the house contains an

interesting mixture of architectural features. It has curved Dutch ogee gables decorated with stone finials, a massive Dutch chimney breast, and an ornate Chinese Chippendale staircase. The house has four fireplaces, including one in an upstairs bedroom. Much of the tiled roof is original, supported by beams of bullit wood and mastic. The original kitchen was built as a separate building to the north of the house to prevent the spread of fire.

The two front rooms are panelled in the now-extinct West Indian cedar once grown locally on the estate. There are many antiques, some of which have stood in the house since the turn of the 19th century. A grandfather clock built in 1759 and a small Sheraton sideboard *circa* 1780 are of particular interest. Perhaps the most intriguing piece, however, is a Victorian reading chair that

looks more like an instrument of torture than one of quiet pleasure.

Outbuildings include the original bath house, lavatory, stables, and saddle-rooms. The gardens in front of the house are well laid-out and include a medieval herb garden and set of coral drip-stones to the right of the entrance porch.

A short film depicting plantation life at St. Nicholas in the mid-1930s is shown twice a day. Cane was ground here until 1947, and the ruins of the syrup factory, windmill, and watermill lie just to the north of the house. The 420-acre (170-hectare) estate still grows cane, but it is now shipped by road to the nearby Portvale Sugar Factory for processing.

Left: The ground floor of St. Nicholas Abbey is furnished with elegant 18th-century furniture. Above: The white gabled Great House of St. Nicholas Abbey.

Welchman Hall Gully

Located off Highway 2, situated close to Harrison's Cave in St. Thomas.

Telephone: 438-6671

Hours: Daily except public holidays, 9am to 5pm

Entrance fee: Reasonable.

Welchman Hall Gully is one of the island's most interesting natural attractions. At one time it was entirely underground and formed part of the network of subterranean chambers known as the Harrison's Cave System. The collapse of the roof and subsequent erosion transformed it from a cave into a ravine. The name originates from General Williams, a Welshman who was the first proprietor of the land in which the gully lies. It was cleared and planted with a variety of tropical trees and flowering plants in the mid-19th century, but fell quickly into neglect and was allowed to grow wild until its purchase by the Barbados National Trust in 1962.

There are over 200 species of plants present in the half-a-mile-long gully, of which close to fifty are clearly numbered. At the northern entrance the gully is wide and flat-bottomed but becomes narrower and more convoluted as you follow the path toward the southern exit. Visitors can, in fact, enter the gully from either end. A well-laid-out path, concrete steps, and handrails make the walk an easy one, and the steep sides and overhead canopy of trees keep the gully pleasantly cool.

Pock-marking the gully walls is a series of caves, which are home to several species of bats whose tell-tale droppings are clearly visible. There are numerous stalactites and stalagmites that in one location have joined to form a pillar almost 5 feet (1.5 metres) in diameter.

Several fine examples of the bearded fig tree – from which the island takes its name (it is called *Los Barbados* in Portuguese; meaning 'the bearded one') – send curtains of aerial roots cascading toward the ground, interwoven with a variety of climbing vines and lianas.

Green monkeys frequent the gully and can often be seen traversing the tree canopy. The spices that grow here include nutmeg and clove; fruits include the golden apple, guava, sweet and sour oranges; and the tree fern – found in very few areas of the island – is one of many of the rarer plant species. Midway along the gully is a magnificent stand of bamboo that towers over a small pond. There is an observation point high up at the northern end of the gully that affords a spectacular view of the east coast and surrounding countryside.

Sunbury Plantation House

Situated on Highway 5, near Six Roads, St. Philip.

Telephone: 423-6270

Fax: 423-5863

Hours: Daily 10am–5pm

Entrance fee: Minimal, with reduced rates for children.

Facilities: Small restaurant and bar; gift shop.

Built around 1660, Sunbury Plantation House is one of the island's oldest and most beautifully restored plantation houses. The entire house is open to the public and gives a comprehensive picture of a bygone Barbados. The ground floor rooms contain beautiful examples of Barbadian antique mahogany furniture, including an ornate 1830 sideboard and an 18-seat dinner table. The study contains planters chairs and a planter's desk – which has been in the house for over 200 years – plus an 1888 bible and an early calculator from 1905. The walls and hallways are adorned with antique maps and prints, including a rare photograph of the old east coast railway taken *circa* 1890. A full suit of armour stands at one end of the drawing room.

Carved four-poster mahogany beds, hand-made Victorian dolls, a marble hip bath and a pair of glass flycatchers are among the hundreds of antiquities contained in the four upstairs bedrooms.

The cellars are also stocked with treasures. The present owner's grandfather was the first optician in Barbados, and a collection of old machines, lenses, instruments, and prints relating to optometry are kept here. The adjoining carriage museum contains several restored horse-drawn carriages and many equestrian accessories.

Sunbury is a living museum, despite the fact that the house was gutted by fire in 1995. All that remained of the building were the coral-stone walls. It took a little over a year to rebuild and refurbish the house, and it was reopened in September of 1996.

The gardens contain an interesting collection of agricultural tools and horse-drawn buggies.

Sunbury offers candlelit dinners in the evenings for groups of up to thirty people.

Top: Sunbury Plantation House is one of the oldest of the island's Great Houses. Centre: The dining room features a magnificent claw-footed dining table. Bottom: The bedrooms are filled with elegant antiques.

Tyrol Cot Heritage Village

Located on Codrington Hill in St. Michael.

Telephone: 424-2074

Hours: Monday to Friday from 9am to 5pm

Entrance fee: Minimal.

Facilities: There is a restaurant on the premises; parking for the village is on the opposite side of the street.

Tyrol Cottage Heritage Village (or 'Tyrol Cot', as it is more commonly known) is the showpiece of the Barbados National Trust. It combines one of the island's most historic buildings with an artists' community housed in traditional Bajan chattel houses. The main house was the home of the late Sir Grantley Adams, an eminent statesman and the only prime minister of the short-lived Federation of the West Indies. It was built in 1854 by local builder William Farnum, who also built Glendairy Prison. It is basically Georgian in design, but contains an interesting mix of architectural oddities. The original roof was designed to catch rain water and was known as a 'fishpond' roof.

There are numerous Roman arches, some beautiful Victorian cast-iron work, and examples of double 'Demerera' windows, an innovation designed to keep the rain out while letting the breeze in. It is furnished with a collection of antiques that have been acquired by the Adams family over the last two centuries. There is some beautiful hand-made locally-crafted mahogany furniture, an impressive collection of china, and an array of African carvings. The book-lined study contains many of Sir Grantley's personal effects, including the flag of the Federation.

The cluster of brightly-painted chattel houses that sit in the well-kept grounds display some of the island's finest arts and crafts. Each building offers a different discipline and operates as a studio as well as a retail outlet. Painting,

leather crafting, needlework, wood carving, pottery, and basket-making are all well represented. The basketry shop features the work of Gloria Gaskin, the 1998 recipient of The 10th International American Award for Quality. Her straw hats and bags have taken the fashion industry by storm around the world.

There is a traditional rum shop offering a variety of Bajan fare, a perfect replica of a blacksmith's shop, and a chattel house museum that depicts a typical 1920s Barbadian home. The old stables adjacent to the main house now house a restaurant that offers both indoor and courtyard dining. Next to this is a faithful replica of an 1820's slave hut complete with its meagre allotment of furnishings.

Above: Tradtional Bajan chattel house in Tyrol Cot Heritage Village.

Atlantis Submarine

Atlantis Submarines is located in Bridgetown at the bottom of Spring Garden Highway.

Telephone: 436-8929

Hours: Varies. Reservations required.

Entrance fee: Costly, but a fabulous experience.

Facilities: Due to restricted access and variable sea conditions the company cannot carry passengers on either of its vessels who are not themselves mobile.

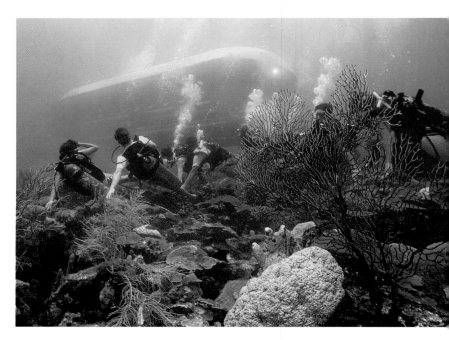

Atlantis Submarines offers a number of fabulous tours in both semi- and fully-submersible craft. The 'Atlantis Expedition' is one-hour tour that is available from Monday through Friday (and, subject to demand, on the occasional weekend).

After watching an orientation video in the reception area, passengers are ferried by shuttle boat to the *Atlantis III*, a forty-eight-seat passenger submarine. Designed and built in Canada, the vessel is certified to operate to a depth of 150 feet (46 metres) and is among a fleet of similar crafts operated by Atlantis in tourist destinations around the world. Thirteen plexiglass viewports line each side of the 65-foot (20-metre) hull, and a curved front viewport neary 5 feet (1.5 metres) in diameter houses the pilot and his controls. Passengers sit back-to-back in two rows, close enough to the viewport to press their nose or camera against it. A co-pilot seated in the stern provides a running commentary on the corals, fish, and other creatures that the submarine encounters on it's journey. Classification charts for fish and coral are located inside the submarine and make for easy identification of the various species.

During the dive, the submarine leaves the top of the reef and drops down to around 115 feet (35 metres) to view the wreck of the *Lord Willoughby*, a small water barge sunk to create an artificial reef and undersea attraction. It sits at the very base of the reef, beyond which the limited amount of sunlight inhibits growth and the seabed slopes away into a ghostly emptiness.

The 'Atlantis Odyssey' dive takes place on Wednesday at 5pm and, in addition to the attractions of the regular tour, it includes a fifteen-minute interactive dive show. At specially designated sites, two scuba divers hand-feed a variety of fish – among them several large green moray eels – which have been become accustomed to this practice over the years. Afterwards, a type of 'underwater dance' takes place as the two divers perform a series of acrobatic manouevres on underwater scooters. They are in direct communication with the submarine for the entire show their commentary is broadcast over the internal PA system.

Atlantis also operates the *Seatrec*, a semi-submersible that offers underwater sightseeing and snorkelling cruises. It can accommodate up to thirty-six passengers, who sit 6 feet (2 metres) below the surface in an air-conditioned glass-walled observatory. Video monitors show live close-up footage of the reef relayed to the vessel by a diver's hand-held camera.

Passengers have a chance to view the *Atlantis III* underwater as it commences its descent into the deep. *Seatrec* tours operate on Tuesdays, Wednesdays and Thursdays, every hour on the hour, from 9am to 1pm. On Fridays it runs snorkelling trips into Carlisle Bay to explore the shallow-water wreck of the *Berywn*. Masks, fins, and snorkels are supplied onboard, and the tours are led by certified diving instructors.

Opposite: Divers, led by certified instructors, surround the Atlantis Submarine as it makes its way through Barbados's coral gardens. Centre: Dazzling reef fish. Right: Fabulous coral formations are home to countless reef rish.

g e

eached!

Where does one start with beaches in Barbados? The island has, without doubt, some of the best and most varied beaches in the Caribbean. Miles of windswept pink or powder white sand make up the flat expanses and secluded coves which surround this jewel of an island. There are too many to mention here, but some of Barbados' best are described below.

All of the beaches on Barbados are in the public domain and cannot be privately owned. Not all beaches, however, have public right-of-way – but there is nothing to stop anybody landing by boat.

Pay careful attention to warning flags on the beach. If the red flag is flying or a lifeguard advises you

not to; **do not swim**. Drownings are by no means unheard of in Barbados, even on the west coast. There are fierce rip currents and undertows on some of the beaches, particularly those on the north and east coasts. Exercise caution and heed local advice when swimming at secluded spots; help may be a long way away.

There are dozens of independent watersports operators who ply their trade on the beaches, offering jet-skis, water-skiing, tube and banana rides, hobie cats, and even parasailing. There are no set rates for any of these activities, so negotiate with the operator to obtain the best price. Establish in advance whether you are dealing in Bajan or US dollars, or it could end up costing you more than you bargained for!

West coast

Just north of Holetown is **Folkstone Park and Marine Reserve** which is operated by the National Conservation Commission. There is a visitor centre that houses a gift shop and marine museum with a small salt-water aquarium. The 2-mile (2.5-km) stretch of Marine Reserve offers excellent snorkelling and beach facilities,

including picnic tables, showers, and washrooms. Snorkelling and scuba equipment are available for hire through the visitor centre, which is open Monday to Friday from 9am–5pm.

The beaches of the **Coral Reef**, **Colony Club, Glitter Bay**, and **Royal Pavillion** are found just to the north of Holetown. These hotel beaches are equipped with sun loungers and umbrellas. They are typical of the west coast with smooth, fine sand, sheltered bays and calm, clear water. Facilities vary from beach to beach, but in general wherever there is a hotel you will find a wide selection of food, drink and watersports.

Opposite: Graceful palms beside the King's Beach Hotel on the west coast. Centre: Barbados has miles of white sandy beaches. Above: Casuarina trees are found on beaches all around the island.

swimming. A reef running perpendicular to the shore separates Mullins and Gibbs bays. It offers superb snorkelling and produces some of the most spectacular surfing conditions during the winter months.

A ten-minute stroll north from Mullins will take you across **Turtle Beach**, **King's Beach,** past the **Sandridge Hotel**, and on to **Cobbler's Cove Hotel**.

North coast

North coast beaches are generally hard to access and are invariably surrounded by high

Continuing north into the parish of St. Peter, the road runs close to **Mullins Beach**, one of the most popular and picturesque of the west coast beaches. The south end of this gently curving bay has a dozen or so lofty casuarina trees which provide a good spot for a picnic. Although a favourite, the beach is seldom crowded as there are very few large hotels this far north. There are several independent watersports operators who ply their trade here and offer water-skiing, tube rides, bananas, jet-skis, and hobie cats. Mullins Beach Bar sits midway along the beach and houses a bar and separate restaurant area. Its open plan

Above: The Caribbean Sea shimmers in the moonlight. Right: Young girl delights in the sun and sand of Barbados.

design and high ceilings ensure a steady through-breeze, and there is no finer place to watch the sun set than from the covered wooden veranda. A pair of brightly-painted gift shops sit adjacent to the bar and sell a wide variety of local arts and crafts. As with all west coast beaches, the sea here is flat and calm and perfect for swimming.

Walk south from Mullins around the sea wall and you will get to **Gibbs Beach**. This is another beautiful west coast location which is very peaceful. There are no hotels – only private houses, and most people miss the beach, as it is tucked away out of sight of the main road. The occasional water-skier may sweep into the bay, but for the most part it is tranquil and serene with fabulous

cliffs. Swimming off this coast is not advisable in certain locations as there are strong currents and the shoreline is generally rocky. However, for the competent swimmer these beaches offer pristine snorkelling. Coral, sea fans and driftwood litter the sands creating a beachcomber's heaven. Remember to heed local advice and exercise caution – you are a long way from any facilities. **Cluffs Bay** in St. Lucy is a beautiful spot, but requires some walking off the beaten track. A four-wheel-drive vehicle will help shorten the distance from the main road, but bring a decent pair of walking shoes as you cannot get down to the beach in flip-flops. Ask for directions – there are well-worn paths, but you need to pick the right one!

Rounding North Point and turning south, there are a few small beaches tucked into the base of the coral cliffs. These face the full force of the Atlantic and again are not for the faint-hearted. The beach at the now-closed North Point Surf Resort is often empty and particularly pretty. Large coral boulders sit about a hundred yards (90 metres) from the beach and, as the name would suggest, the surfing is good. Continuing south-east

around the coastline, **River Bay** is popular with locals and can be easily reached by road. Here the river mouth provides a sheltered cut in the cliffs, but swimming is not advised. There are washroom facilities, a bus stop, and a local restaurant/rum shop is nearby.

East coast

Continuing south around the coastline, you enter the parish of St. Andrew and arrive at **Morgan Lewis Beach**. This is one of the most spectacular beaches on the island and runs uninterrupted for over 5 miles (8 km), from **Pico Tenerife** in St. Andrew to **Cattlewash** in St. Joseph. Totally unspoiled and undeveloped, it has changed little since the island was discovered.

A constant train of Atlantic breakers crash onto the beach, and the wind whips up clouds of spray that drift gently inland. Huge piles of driftwood, coconuts, and assorted flotsam cover the beach – providing more spoils for the beachcomber. It is interesting to stop and consider where these things might have come from, as there is nothing out there but 3,000 miles (4,800 km) of open sea.

Right: The tranquil waters of the west coast of Barbados.

Access to the beach is limited as there are few roads that run close to it. To enter from the north, drive down Cherry Tree Hill, past Morgan Lewis windmill and farm, and continue to a palm-lined cart track off to the left at the bottom of the hill. Drive down here – only if you have a four-wheel-drive vehicle – to the north end of the beach. Access at the southern end is just south of Belleplaine on the East Coast Road (Ermy Bourne Highway). There are several tracks going off into the dunes on the left-hand side of the road just south of the village. Park at the end of the track, climb over the dunes, and you are on the beach.

Barclays Park marks the end of Morgan Lewis Beach and is a favourite spot for family outings. Swimming here is still not advisable. Several wooden picnic

Above: Fabulous Crane Beach is a perfect spot for body surfing and boogie-boarding. Right: Children play on Silver Sands beach in the south of the island.

tables are set back from the beach, situated in the shade of the delicate casuarina trees. There are both shower and washroom facilities, and the adjoining **Barclays Park Restaurant** offers a good selection of hot and cold meals and a fully-stocked bar.

Pass Cattlewash and go up to the top of the hill, turn immediately left, and descend steeply into the fishing village of **Bathsheba.** Here huge coral boulders sit in the water, and hard-core surfers ride the waves of the 'Soup Bowl'. This is *the* place to surf, but you have to be good – it is definitely not for beginners. Low tide exposes large rock pools just below the Roundhouse, and since there are very few places to swim on the east coast they provide one of the only places you can cool off in comfort. Your own rock pool, a cold beer, and a good book – life just does not get much better than that. The Edgewater Inn, the Roundhouse, and the Bonito Bar all have good restaurants, and there are several local rum shops in the village.

Tent Bay, **Martin's Bay**, and **Congor Bay** are all fishing villages on this side of the island and, although picturesque, do not have much in the way of beaches. However, the next village, **Bath,** is a popular Sunday destination – featuring a park with picnic tables and washroom facilities. There is fabulous snorkelling over an extensive reef system.

South-east coast

Continue south past **Consett Bay** and the lighthouse at Ragged Point, past **Skeetes Bay** and on to **Bottom Bay** in the parish of St. Philip. Protected by a ring of high

cliffs, this beautiful white-sand beach is one of the loveliest on the island. A small grove of coconut trees provides a shady spot, and further down the beach the sea has eroded the cliff face to form a huge cavern that is large enough to contain a small house. The water here is an azure blue, and a lively swell makes for great body-surfing. Access is via a steep flight of steps at the south end of the beach. There are a couple of picnic tables in the lee of the cliff and, more often than not, the beach is empty.

Further south is **Crane Beach,** another beautiful spot. Its fine pink sand is powder soft, and the waters in the sweeping bay are the deepest blue. Perched on the high cliffs at the north end of the beach sits the Crane Beach Hotel, with superb ocean views and a stairway leading down to the water below. A look-out point near the base of the cliffs provides a great diving platform for the adventurous swimmer. The waves here can be huge, and the beach is well-known for body-surfing and boogie-boarding. (Boogie-boards are usually available for rent at the north end

Right: A wide range of watersports facilities are available throughout the island.

of the beach). There are no facilities as such, but the Crane Beach Hotel provides all the amenities normally associated with a good-sized hotel. They charge an entrance fee which is redeemable at the bar if you choose to enter the beach via the hotel. Alternately, there is a clearly-marked access road at the south end of the beach.

A little further north is **Foul Bay**. The road leads almost to the water's edge, where you can stroll along the soft white sands in virtual seclusion.

South coast

Every year some of the best windsurfers in the world descend on **Silver Sands** in Christ Church for the Barbados leg of the world cup circuit. Strong steady winds and large swells make for near-perfect conditions, particularly suited to wave-jumping. Boards are available for rent and lessons can be arranged. A restaurant sits right on the beach and offers a good selection of food, drinks, and windsurfing gossip.

Passing Oistins and heading north leads to **Dover Beach**, one of the island's most popular, and hence most crowded, beaches. Its flat sands are located at the south end of St. Lawrence Gap. There is good swimming and many hotels and restaurants can be found in this area. Charles' Watersports operates from Dover Beach and offers surf bikes, kayaks, hobie cats, and sunfish sailboats. There is a picnic area with washroom facilities and a vendors' market adjacent to the car park.

Accra Beach in Worthing is another busy south coast beach. Sun loungers can be hired, and the watersports hut offers surfboards, boogie boards, hobie cats, sunfish sailboats and snorkelling equipment. The beach is good for swimming and great for people-watching. A vendors'

Far left: Sandy Beach is a popular spot on the south of the island. Left: Golden sunset over the west coast.

Picnic tables, showers, and washrooms are among the facilities, and a range of watersports equipment is available for hire through the bar, including pedal bikes, sun umbrellas, windsurfers and snorkelling equipment.

One last stop before arriving back at Holetown is **Paynes Bay**. Park close to the Coach House and look for the public access to the beach on the opposite side of the road. Walk south past the Treasure Beach and Tamarind Cove hotels to Bombas, a beach bar and restaurant. Further south at the end of the bay is a fish market, where you can watch the daily catch being unloaded and select the freshest of fish.

market sells souvenirs, local crafts, and tasty food. Pay a visit to 'Mad Dog', a leatherworker who makes fabulous shoes and sandals at the side of the road next to the beach.

A little further north is **Sandy Beach**, a flat expanse of white sand popular with both tourists and locals. The nearby reef has created a shallow, sheltered lagoon perfect for relaxation. Sun loungers and snorkelling equipment are available for rent, and the popular Carib Beach Bar offers good food and drinks. It is often the venue for beach volleyball competitions, live music, and general merriment.

Carlisle Bay, just south of Bridgetown, is effectively the city's beach, and runs for about one mile (1.5 km) south from the Careenage to the Hilton Hotel on

Needham's Point. The Carlisle Bay Centre offers shopping, dining, and watersports including glass-bottom boat trips out to the wreck of the *Berwyn*, a French tugboat sunk in 1919. The waters of the bay are calm and sheltered and are now part of a designated Marine Reserve. The lively Boatyard Bar and Restaurant sits right on the beach and offers towels, chairs, cabanas, and snorkelling equipment for rent.

Brighton Beach runs alongside the Spring Garden Highway and is another long expanse of white sand. It is sheltered and provides great swimming. The lively Weiser's Beach Bar is set in a cool, wooded area of the beach.

Above: Barbados provides many places to sit in solitude and relax. Right: Bird's-eye view of the east coast.

wate

The first landfall for many trans-Atlantic sailors are the sun-drenched shores of Barbados, since it is the most easterly island in the Caribbean. There is a wide variety of facilities on offer to visiting yachtsman.

Haul-out and storage facilities are available through Willie's Diving & Marine Services (Tel: 425-1060) at the Shallow Draft Harbour. A tammy-lift can take boats up to 45 tonnes (50 tons), with a maximum 17-foot (5-metre) beam and 7-foot (2-metre) draft. Their wet dock (pontoon) can accomodate a boat up to 48 feet (15 metres) in length and provides minimal electricity which is enough to charge batteries, but not to run air-conditioning units. They supply jacks and props, and will put a boat in position on the hard after it has been hauled out. They also offer long-term storage if required but their rates increase every month if you choose to be there long term. They also offer a pressure washing service.

Carlisle Bay is a favourite anchorage with many yachting enthusiasts and provides a wide range of marine services through two conveniently-placed waterfront businesses. The Boatyard (Tel: 436-2622) offers a daily garbage collection, laundry

vorld

facilities, telephone and fax services, showers, water and ice, and gas bottle refills on Mondays, Wednesdays, and Fridays. Further south is Bay Marine Ltd. (Tel: 228-4720), who specialise in various mechanical repairs, including woodworking, fibreglass and epoxy repairs, aluminium and stainless steel welding. Outboard and Autohelm repairs and servicing are also available.

Both the Boatyard and Bay Marine offer sail repairs, or you can deal directly with Doyle Sails (Tel: 423-4600), who offer a pick-up and delivery service.

Racing

There is a lively racing season in Barbados that kicks off with a round-the-island race in January. A series of round-the-buoys and offshore races follows on Saturdays and Sundays until September, when most of the boats are pulled out of the water. The big event, however, is the Mount Gay Regatta held in May, the last on the annual circuit of Caribbean regattas. This attracts both a regular group of rivals from the islands and new competitors from further afield. The Barbados Yacht Club (Tel: 427-1125) on Lower Bay Street organises most of the races during the season and is a good place to go if you are looking to crew. Racers, cruisers, and dinghies all participate – including some beautiful locally-built wooden boats belonging to members of the Cruising Club, located just south of the Yacht Club in Aquatic Gap.

Most races have a corporate sponsor and are followed by a brief prize-giving and a long free 'happy hour' at the Yacht Club bar. The Yacht Club offers temporary memberships to visiting sailors, who can also then enjoy the club's facilities – such as tennis, croquet, and the beach bar. There is an active youth yachting programme that runs through July and August.

Charters

For those who prefer a more leisurely pace, there are numerous sailboats available for charter. Multi-hulls range from the 70-foot (21-metre) *Tiami II* (Tel: 427-7245) that can carry over 100 people, to *Sinbad*, a 30-foot (9-metre) owner-operated trimaran (Tel: 432-1615). Several mono-hulls are available for charter, including *Secret Love*, a 41-foot (12-metre) Morgan (Tel: 432-1972); *Limbo Lady*, a 44-foot (13-metre) CSY (Tel: 420-5418); and *Regent One*, a 43-foot (13-metre) Beneteau (Tel: 228-1864). Morning, afternoon, and evening cruises are available on most boats, but be sure to check with individual operators. Most cruises include a stop for snorkelling and lunch – one of the most popular spots being adjacent to the shallow wreck of the *Berwyn* in

Carlisle Bay. Another interesting stop is at an area close to the Lone Star Restaurant in St. James, where several resident hawksbill turtles can be hand-fed in the water.

For the serious party animal the four-hour daytime cruise on the *Jolly Roger* is a must. Since its inception almost thirty years ago, enough rum punch has been served on board to float three large cruise liners! These 100-foot (30-metre) wooden brigantines crank up their mega-watt sound systems and set sail for Holetown where a buffet lunch is served at the mooring. A shuttle carries people to the nearby beach if they want to spend a little time ashore, while on board the rope swing and the plank are deployed. A 'pirate wedding' and other surprises are sure to follow, and then it is back down the coast to the port. More sedate evening cruises are also available. Telephone 436-6264 for details.

By far the largest and most unique of all the vessels that ply the waters of Barbados is the *Harbour Master*. This leviathan is 100 feet (30 metres) long, 40 feet (12 metres) wide and has three decks above water. The top deck is open and is kitted out with chairs, tables, sun loungers and a bar. The middle deck hosts evening entertainment, including theatre productions, floor shows, and live music. The bottom deck has a wrap-around bar that can seat 120 people – making it the largest floating bar in the Caribbean. A huge bow ramp can be lowered to the beach to let passengers disembark and spend time ashore, and a curved water-slide runs from the top deck to some 10 feet (3 metres) above the water. Below the water-line are fresh-water showers and washrooms, a gift shop, a 1950s theme cocktail lounge, and a semi-submersible. Seating twenty-nine people, the latter is lowered down from the belly of the ship on hydraulic rams and offers a fish-eye view of the world below. The vessel then hovers above an established feeding station on the reef as a pair of divers take to the water in what is billed as an 'interactive dive show'. Accustomed to this daily ritual, hundreds of fish immediately surround the divers just feet from the observation windows. The *Harbour Master* offers other fun-filled activities, including dances, sunset cruises, beach trips, live entertainment, and private functions. Telephone 430-0900 for details.

Island hopping

For those who may wish to venture further afield and visit some of the neighbouring islands by boat, there are many options. A crossing to the Grenadines – some 100 miles (160 km) to the west – takes around twelve to sixteen hours, depending on weather conditions and the size of the boat. A following wind and calm seas make comfortable sailing, and on a clear, starry night the passage is very beautiful. Once in the Grenadines, island-hopping is easy, and the area contains some of the most spectacular cruising grounds in the world. Several local operators offer cruises to the Grenadines from Barbados; the norm is to sail down and fly back (sailing back can be quite arduous, as you are heading into the wind and waves all the way up). You can also fly down, pick up a yacht in the

Grenadines, and fly back. Chantours (Tel: 432-5591) offers a variety of day tours and can also arrange live-aboard charters in the region.

Ocean Mist is a purpose-built 60-foot (18-metre) power catamaran designed for inter-island travel in style and comfort. It has four air-conditioned double cabins, each with their own shower and toilet. Other facilities include a full bar and galley, a large saloon, a sun deck, and a covered fly bridge. All customs, health and immigration procedures are handled by the crew – all you need is your passport. When not on charter outside of Barbados, *Ocean Mist* is available for coastal cruises,

parties and cocktail parties. Telephone 436-7639 for details.

One of the more adventurous means of inter-island travel is onboard the *M.V. Windward*, a 180-foot (55-metre) passenger ferry offering services within the Eastern Caribbean and to the South American mainland. Reasonably priced, trips range from a weekend in St. Lucia with optional accomodation on board to a six-day trip calling at St. Vincent, Trinidad, and Venezuela. The boat can accommodate up to seventy passengers and offers duty-free shopping, a restaurant, bar, and television lounge. Details on cruises are available from Windward Agencies at 431-0499.

underwate

extravaganza

Endless sunshine, palm-fringed beaches, balmy tropical nights... it all adds up to a heady cocktail of Barbadian perfection. But visitors to this tiny coral cornucopia of holiday delights are starting to discover that one of the best-kept secrets of Barbados is hidden beneath its warm turquoise waters.

Until recently, little was known about Barbados' pristine reefs, numerous wrecks and world-class dive facilities. The warm waters that surround the island provide the quintessential environment for the life of a reef. Here tiny coral polyps proliferate, building upon the limestone skeletons of their ancestors to provide numerous habitats for a biological diversity of exotic and colourful species, that is equally as fragile as the great rainforests of the world'.

Each side of the island offers new adventures and marine life. From the rugged east coast standing solid against the power of the Atlantic Ocean, with its walls, caverns, and vast submerged boulders, to the passive blue waters of the west coast, with its Plato-like reefs of soft curves. In between lies the south coast, with its miles of barrier reefs, good drift dives, and busy marine life. The island has two basic reef structures: the fringing or patching reefs, which are near shore and almost surround the island, and the barrier reefs (also called banking reefs) scattered on the south and west coasts.

Fringing reefs

Though accessible as shore dives, most of these near-shore sites are not clearly marked and, from time to time, have long-shore currents. (Boat diving is recommended for most, if not all Barbados' dive sites.) Shallower sections of these reefs, 25 feet (8 metres) or less are largely covered with sea fans and brown gorgonians, which give way to a variety of hard and soft corals

around the 40-foot (12-metre) mark. While these reefs are not as magnificent or as pristine as the barrier reefs, they are busy nurseries for hundreds of small tropical fish. Typical depth range here is 20 to 60 feet (6 to 18 metres), and marine life of interest includes frogfish, flying gunards, snake eels, stingrays, eagle rays, and sea-horses.

Inner reefs are generally taken as the second dive of the day, but those who dive them as a first dive will find plenty of variety between the sites.

Opposite: Parrotfish, well-named for their bright colours, are often seen nibbling on limestone corals. Top: Scuba diver admires the incredible coral formations on Barbados' pristine reefs. Centre: The delicate Christmas tree tube worm.

These are computer-assisted dives, with a Beginner to Intermediate level depth and bottom time range from 30 feet (9 metres) to 60 feet (18 metres) for between thirty-five and fifty-five minutes. As with all other dives, air checks are at 1500 *psi* (100 bar) and 750 *psi* (50 bar), with a minimum of 650 *psi* (45 bar) reserved for the ascent. A word of caution: the outer edges of some of these reefs drop to well below 60 feet (18 metres), so it is important to keep watch on your depth, especially if this is your second dive of the day.

Barrier reefs

These are definitely boat dives, being between one quarter to 2 miles (0.5 to 3 km) from the shore. These impressive reefs are common on the south coast – and usually run parallel to the shore. They can be as little as 30 feet (9 metres) across and one mile (1.5 km) long. Large corals of just about every type fight for space with sponges, sea whips, deep-water gorgonians, and sea fans. Here, shaped by currents, convoluted barrel sponges have taken the shape of enormous

The Friar's Craig, a 170-foot (52-metre) freighter sunk in 1985, lies just offshore in 50 feet (15 metres) of water between two reefs. Whether you start or end your dive here, this well-encrusted wreck has abundant life to explore. **Close Encounters** is a shallow reef just one minute's boat ride from the nearest dive shop. This is *Exploresub's* famous 'fish-feeding' dive, where visitors can feed 'Sarge', a southern Caribbean stingray, as well as moray eels and a wide variety of tropical fish.

Church Point, **Peter's Paradise** and **The Boot** provide a great chance to see some magnificent eagle rays and turtles. These reefs run parallel to shore, and drift-diving the outer edge where it meets the sand allows divers to keep a look-out in the deeper water to see what swims past.

clams, providing shelter for banded coral shrimp, spiny crabs, basket starfish, as well as enormous ancient brain coral.

With a typical depth range of 60 to over 140 feet (18 to over 43 metres), the hawksbill and green turtle are commonly seen here. Large pelagic fish are also visitors to these reefs. During the summer months, baitfish in their thousands form dark wave-like clouds across these reefs, sometimes engulfing divers and obscuring the sun. Mantas and even whale sharks have been seen – but are by no means common.

The minimum depth on most barrier reefs is around 65 feet

(20 metres), although some of them (like those on the south coast) may be as little as 35 feet (11 metres) across the top. They may have almost vertical walls and can be subject to strong currents.

In general, these reefs are in pristine condition, with large coral heads, sponges, and plant life. Tropicals and larger predators can be found here. Turtles are almost a certainty and are quite tame. Most of these reefs are found in depths of 200 feet (61 metres) or more.

Some of these reefs such as **Muff, Ernie's Bar**, and **Castle Bank** are good for drift diving.

Depth and bottom time is usually 60–90 feet (18–27 metres); twenty-seven to thirty-two minutes. Most dives are multi-level, with a safety stop at 15–25 feet (5–8 metres) for four to six minutes.

All divers are required to give air checks at 1500 and 750 *psi*, with a minimum of 650 *psi*

reserved for the ascent and safety stop.

These are some of the healthiest reefs in the Caribbean – but watch for reefs that dip and climb like saw teeth, which can predispose you to decompression sickness when doing computer assisted multi-level profiles. Most barrier reefs drop past the 140-foot (43-metre) mark before they start to thin out to sand, so always watch your depth.

Top left: Grunts shimmer against the wreck of the Berwyn which lies within the Carlisle Bay Marine Park. Centre: The endangered hawksbill turtle is a regular visitor to the barrier reefs in Barbados. Above: Graceful seahorses are prolific on the fringing reefs which surround Barbados.

Wrecks

Barbados boasts more than seventeen wrecks and is considered by many to be the 'wreck diving capital of the Caribbean'. Only nine wrecks are dived on a regular basis, as some lie on the south-east coast where conditions are apt to be on the rough side. Others are beyond the recreational diving limits.

Most wrecks are within 50 feet (15 metres) of the surface. Some, such as the **Berwyn,** (also spelt Berwind), which lies within the Carlisle Bay Marine Park (see 'Marine Parks', overleaf), is a mere 8 feet (2 metres) from the surface. **MV Eillon**, also in the park, is 52 feet (16 metres) at its stern and 15 feet (5 metres) from the surface. The **SS Stavronikita** is Barbados' premier wreck and is rated among the world's top ten. The Greek freighter was gutted by a fire in the mid-seventies, and only after three terrifying days adrift were the crew rescued and the 365-foot (111-metre) vessel towed to Barbados. Three years later, in November 1978, the 'Stavro' as locals refer to it was sunk in less than seventeen minutes. An impressive sight and a professional display of know-how by a team of demolition experts,

who dispelled all concerns that this monster of a ship might tip over on its side: twenty years later, it still sits perfectly upright on its keel.

The maximum depth on the *Stavro* is 127 feet (39 metres) at its prop. Its forward mast reaches to within 18 feet (5 metres) of the surface; its smokestack and wheelhouse are at 55 and 65 feet (17 and 20 metres) respectively.

After almost twenty years on the ocean floor, this wreck has been transformed into a hive of activity. Its hull is gilded with sea whips, soft and hard corals, sponges, and gorgonians. Its masts and upper cabins swarm with sergeant majors, tangs, blue cromis, and red hinds. Among others, barracuda, mackerel, and turtles are common visitors to the wreck.

There are seventeen profiles that take you through the cabins and hull, ranging from Open Water to Advanced and Wreck Speciality certification levels. Profile seventeen is

multi-level and computer-assisted. The maximum depth at Intermediate level is 100 feet (30 metres), while the average depth is 70 feet (21 metres).

The bottom time is twenty-three minutes, with a safety stop at 15-25-five feet (5 to 8 metres) for five minutes. Air checks are at 1500 *psi* (100 bar) and 750 *psi* (50 bar). The dive ends with a minimum of 650 *psi* (45 bar) or time, whichever comes first. A typical dive starts on the top of the ship's forward mast and travels through cabins and cargo

Opposite: Scuba diver examines part of a wreck and its glorious coral colonies. Below: Scuba diver swims amidst dazzling fan and soft corals.

holds to the maximum depth of 100 feet (30 metres) at the stern cabin. Descent is along the mooring line, which is anchored near to the top of the mast.

Another word of caution: all dives on the *Stavro* should be made under the direct supervision of a certified instructor. You should never enter an overhead area with less than a third of your air supply remaining in your cylinder. There should be an exit point within 15 feet (5 metres) of you at all times. Do not enter into passageways or cabins unless you can see your exit point. Do not hold onto water pipes or any parts of the ceiling, as this can cause objects to fall on you.

Background: The reefs in Barbados are a fantasy world filled with a kaleidoscopic variety of colour, shape and form. It is here that the rich diversity of nature is displayed with spectacular effect. Above: Sharp nose puffer. Right: Colourful anemones of the coral reefs.

Marine Parks

Barbados has two marine parks – Folkestone Marine Park on the west coast and Carlisle Bay Marine Park south of Bridgetown.

Folkestone Marine Park is interesting despite the fact that the coral has been eroded by storm surges over the past few years. This is a good area for snorkelling with depths of 5 to 25 feet (1.5 to 8 metres).

South of Bridgetown, Carlisle Bay was the hub for cargo ships during the 17th century and was an active harbour up until the late 1950s and early 1960s. Over 200 hundred ships were lost in the bay during this time. Though few have been found, four wrecks – the *Berwyn*, *Eillon*, *C-Treck* and *Fox* – are all located close to each other and make up the major attractions of the **Carlisle Bay Marine Park**. While most of the life is found on the wrecks, there are many rare species to be found on the sandy flats and small shrubs including seahorses, flying gurnard, batfish, frogfish, and giant sand eels. This area is ideal for macro- and wide-angle photography and makes for a great night dive.

The *Berwyn* is a French tug which sank in 1919 under mysterious circumstances. One story reports that the vessel was fired on by a German destroyer but made it safely to the shallow waters of Carlisle Bay where it sunk during the night. The *Berwyn* is 70 feet (21 metres) long and sits at its stern in 21 feet (6 metres) of water, with her most shallow point some 8 feet (2 metres) from the surface.

One of two wrecks that was deliberately sunk is the *Eillon* which went down in June 1996. Boarded by the Barbados Coast Guard six years earlier, it was found to have a quantity of illegal drugs hidden onboard. It was impounded and subsequently environmentally prepared before being sunk in the park. The *Eillon* sits in 53 feet (16 metres) of water at its stern and is 15 feet (5 metres) from the surface at its shallowest point. An amazing amount of marine life has taken to the hull in the short time it has been underwater.

Built for use as a fishing vessel, the 46-foot (14-metre) *C-Treck* sits in 43 feet (13 metres) of water. Its concrete hull is home to many crustaceans, and moray eels of all sizes live here.

Only the keel and rudder section of the *Fox* remains. Copper and brass spikes can still be seen protruding from its wooden planks. Some small fish and the occasional seahorse can be found here. This dive is profiled at Beginner and Intermediate levels.

The average depth in the park is 25 feet (8 metres), with a maximum depth reached on the *Eillon* at 53 feet (16 metres). Bottom time is not a factor if the deeper wrecks are done first, since much of the dive will be spent on the *Berwyn* in less than 25 feet (8 metres). However, if you are on a repetitive dive, you will need to pay attention to the depth at the *Berwyn*, as it is so close to the surface. Air checks are, as always, at 1500 *psi* (100 bar) and 750 *psi* (50 bar), with a minimum of 500 *psi* (40 bar) reserved for your return to the surface.

Take care as the bottom consists of mainly sandy areas that are heavily used. It is therefore essential to position yourself so as to avoid stirring up the bottom.

General facts

Visibility in Barbados' waters generally averages from 40 to 60ft (12 to18 metres), but is at its best during the summer months, when it can reach up to 100 ft (30 metres). Water temperatures average between 82 and 85°F (27 and 29°C).

In terms of facilities, Barbados has one decompression chamber, which is situated at St. Ann's Fort, midway between the major dive sites. It is staffed twenty-four hours a day by two full-time doctors, trained in hyperbaric medicine and backed up by defense force personnel.

floral

fiesta

A visitor to Barbados some four centuries ago would have found a very different-looking island indeed: one blanketed in dense tropical forest with little in the way of open pastures. The advent of the sugar industry changed all this, and within a few decades most of the native forest had been cleared to allow for the cultivation of sugar cane. The island is geologically younger, flatter, and drier than its volcanic neighbours and has never enjoyed the same biodiversity.

It is believed that most of Barbados' first plants arrived from the islands directly to the south and from the South American mainland. A smaller number are thought to have come from the islands to the north, and some even from Africa. The tradewinds, marine life, ocean currents and birds all bore seeds and seed pods to the island. The ubiquitous **coconut palm** originated in the Pacific and Indian oceans, but its seeds after floating thousands of miles across the open seas, washed up on the beaches of the Caribbean. Man subsequently introduced many species, some of which have become naturalised and flourish in the wild; others are only found in carefully-tended gardens.

Many of the flowers and trees typically associated with the Caribbean are not native to the islands. The **flamboyant tree** was introduced from Madagascar; the **casuarina** is a native of Australia; the **African tulip tree** comes from West Africa, and the **tamarind tree** originates in the Far East. **Bougainvillea** was brought to Barbados from Brazil, **hibiscus** from Hawaii, and **allamanda** from Guyana. The ornamental **Pride of Barbados**, is believed to originate in South America It bears bright clusters of fiery red or yellow flowers with long, projecting stamens. Perhaps the most famous import of all is the **breadfruit tree**, introduced to the Caribbean in 1793 by Captain Bligh of *Mutiny on the Bounty* fame. Certainly the most famous indigenous species is the **grapefruit** which originated in Barbados and is a hybrid of the sour orange and the shaddock.

Today there are some 700 species of flowering plant in Barbados and several markedly differing ecosystems.

Top left: The dazzling ixora is a common sight in Barbados. Top right: The Flower Forest is host to many glorious flowers and shrubs. Bottom left: Many species of orchid flourish in Barbados. Bottom right: The national flower is the 'Pride of Barbados'. Right: The beautiful hibiscus is a symbol of the tropics.

Barbadian gullies

There are over 100 miles (161 km) of gullies in the island which are fissures in the coral cap that in some places reach depths of nearly 200 feet (61 metres). They are covered in dense vegetation and are an integral part of the island's natural drainage system. For the most part they are untouched by man. The obstruction of one such gully led to catastrophic floods in 1995 when torrential rains burst a blocked bridge and sent thousands of tons of water crashing down a gully and into the village of Weston in St. James. Some dozen houses were destroyed, cars were washed out to sea, and one man tragically lost his life.

Aerial roots and hanging vines reach down in great swathes toward the gully floor, and giant coral boulders and dimly-lit caves provide refuge for many species of flora and fauna alike. The shady humid conditions are ideal for the growth of many plants,

particularly ferns and mosses, which are found in great abundance. Together with **Turner's Hall Wood**, the gullies of Barbados best represent the island's natural vegetation and have changed little over the centuries. Both the National Trust (Tel: 426-2421 or 436-9033) and the Future Centre Trust (Tel: 425-2020) have a programme of hikes that take in some of the island's best gullies. Of particular interest is **Welchman Hall Gully**, near Harrison's Cave, one of Barbados' most interesting natural attractions (*see Sightseeing Spectacular, page 53*).

Above: Rich shades of bougainvillea grace streets and gardens throughout the island. Centre: Delicate crimson orchid in the Flower Forest. Opposite: The yellow allamanda is a common ornamental shrub which originates from Brazil.

Arid lands

The drier coastal regions of the island support a different type of plant life. Here you will find the **century plant**, or maypole (*agave barbadensis*) one of the three plant species native to Barbados. Looking much like a cactus, it has a ring of large, sharp-tipped leaves at its base and a tall central stalk that bears bright yellow flowerheads. It takes at least ten years for the plant to flower, which probably explains the first of its common names. Where the second originates is unknown, but it would be fair to assume that it was a reminder to the early settlers of a maypole.

The coastal area near Morgan Lewis Beach in St. Andrew is particularly rich in cacti and has an abundance of species.

Examples include the century plant, **prickly pear** (known locally as the flat-hand pimploe), **Turk's cap**, **Peruvian apple cactus**, an endemic species of columnar cactus, and many varieties of agave – one of which is often seen in front of chattel houses, its sharp tips decorated with egg shells. Common to all coastal areas is the **sea grape**, which grows along the fringe of the beaches and bears an edible fruit that is similar to the wine grape.

Forest and wetland flora

Turner's Hall Wood in St. Andrew is one of the few remaining areas of virgin forest and contains the highest concentration of plant species on the island – many of which are found only in this location. The 74-acre (30-hectare) wood contains both deciduous and evergreen trees and is properly termed a semi-deciduous or mesophytic forest. There are three canopy levels. The species forming the top canopy some, 100 feet (30 metres) up, include the locust tree; the sandbox tree, with its sharp protective spikes; the silk cotton tree, with its massive root buttresses; the trumpet tree; and the fiddle wood. The middle canopy spans the 35- to 65-foot (10- to 20-metre) range and harbours **wild**

cherry, **fustic**, **Spanish oak**, and the **Jack-in-the-box** tree. The third layer, some 15 to 30 feet (4.5 to 9 metres) high, includes the **white harklis**, the **birch gum**, and the **macaw palm**. The latter has thousands of very sharp needles radiating from the trunk and is endemic to the island. The top of Turner's Hall Wood affords magnificent views across the east coast and although it is a steep climb to get up there it is well worth the effort.

Most of the island's coastal wetlands have disappeared with the notable exception of the 90-acre (36-hectare) **Graeme Hall Bird Sanctuary** on the island's south coast. Bordered by a thriving mangrove swamp, this unique eco-sysytem is a world unto itself and supports myriad plantlife and animal species. It is open to the public daily from 7am until 6pm. (see *Wild Things, page 87*).

Two of the island's prime attractions for flower-lovers are the **Andromeda Botanical Gardens** and the **Flower Forest**. The former has one of the finest collections of tropical plants anywhere in the Caribbean, as well as a fabulous palm garden. The ancient **bearded fig tree** is worth seeking out. The 50-acre (20-hectare) Flower Forest offers serene walks through a variety of indigenous and imported plants and trees. (*See Sightseeing Spectacular, pages 39 and 44*).

There are two further avenues of exploration for gardening enthusiasts. **The Barbados Horticultural Society** (Tel: 428-5889) offers an annual programme of 'Open Gardens', allowing public access to some of the most beautiful private gardens in the country – and indeed the Caribbean – for one day of the year. There is a small admission charge, which includes light refreshments.

The **Barbados National Trust** (Tel: 436-9033) offers a similar and very popular 'Open House' programme, where visitors can explore some of the island's loveliest private homes and their lush gardens.

Floral Folklore

Almost as old as the island itself is the ancient tradition of herbal remedies. Since the days of the original Arawak inhabitants, the island's plants have yielded medicine and hopes of life. The African slaves brought their folk cures and bush remedies, and more recently, Rastafarians have extended the beliefs in non-traditional teas.

Some folk cures stem from magical beliefs, highly influenced by the practice of *obeah, (see The Barbados Experience page 31),* a type of witchcraft which originates in West Africa. Today, herbal remedies are gaining popularity amongst Bajans and the range of folk medicines is on the increase.

Thyme and mint are basic cures for stomach discomfort and **ginger** is also used to relieve an unsettled stomach. This is a favorite remedy of fishermen when dealing with anybody suffering from seasickness.

Top left: The sweet-smelling frangipani is a small cultivated tree with large clusters of aromatic flowers. Centre: The Pride of Barbados. Bottom: Exquisite orchids thrive in the Flower Forest. Left: The Andromeda Gardens is home to an outstanding array of palms including the sealing wax palm. Right: Dainty orchid.

Coconut water is hailed as a cure for bladder and kidney ailments, while coconut oil is rubbed into the head to break a cold.

It is claimed that **peanuts** increase sexual activity and tea produced from a bush called **finger-grow** is supposed to work as an aphrodisiac.

The **pawpaw** is used as a laxative as well as for lowering blood pressure. The juice of its stem, roots and leaves is used in the treatment of warts and boils. It is also used for its antiseptic qualities in stopping infection from cuts and bruises.

The **aloe** plant that grows wild throughout the island is a succulent used to treat sunburn and is often among the wares offered by beach vendors. The fleshy leaves are broken open and the jelly inside is applied directly to the skin. Virtually all after-sun products contain aloe. It is also used locally as a tea to cure colds.

The **hog plum** is referred to as a 'cure-all'. The Caribs prepared a tea from the seeds or leaves to soothe sore throats and made leaf poultices to treat sores. It was subsequently used to treat venereal disease, dysentery, and opthalmia.

The **periwinkle,** or 'Old Maid', is a native of Madagascar and was used by the Caribs to treat diabetes. Much more recently it has been used to treat some forms of leukaemia and has been studied as a potential weapon in the fight against cancer.

The **prickly pear** cactus had a number of uses. The stems were peeled and boiled in salt water to treat ulcers and gripe, while the leaves were sliced and then baked to treat headaches.

The extremely hard wood of the **sea grape** was used by the Caribs to make weapons, and the bark is used to treat diarrhoea. **Wild basil** is used in the home to keep out mosquitoes, and both the **trumpet tree** and the **silver bush** were used in the treatment of kidney ailments.

Barbados has a great variety of wildlife. At first glance this might not appear to be the case as there are few large wild animals – certainly none of the big game species. However, closer inspection and careful attention will reveal a wonderful world of smaller, but no less interesting, inhabitants. Some are native, some are unique to the island, and some have been imported from distant continents.

As darkness falls one of the first things you will notice is the hypnotic song of the **cricket** and the **whistling frog**, clearly audible over the telephone to callers thousands of miles away who invariably ask 'What is that noise?' Both these creatures are reclusive and seldom seen, and both possess the knack of suddenly ceasing their song just when you think you have pinpointed their exact location.

Another nocturnal creature is the **bat.** There are six species resident in Barbados, of which two are endemic. They include fish-eating bats, fruit bats, and housebats. They live in attics,

Top: Green monkeys were first brought to Barbados in the 1600s as pets of slave traders. They are prolific throughout the interior of the island. Left: Toucan in Barbados Wildlife Reserve.

belfries, gullies and caves; the largest colonies residing in the undeveloped sections of the **Harrison's Cave** system. Cole's Cave, which ultimately connects with its commercial neighbour, teems with tens of thousands of these creatures, and great mounds of guano carpet the floors of the cave's lightless chambers. Emerging at dusk to feed, bats can often be seen swooping low over swimming pools to scoop up water and insects from the surface.

Barbados has five species of lizard, the most common being the **green lizard** (*anolis*) which lives mostly outdoors. The almost translucent **gecko** (*phyllodactylus pulcher*), is happier indoors and is often seen darting to and fro on ceilings in pursuit of small insects. Both of these creatures are unique to Barbados. Other reptilian residents include the world's smallest snake, the 'blind' or 'worm' snake, and the racer snake, another species found only in Barbados. Neither is harmless but the chance of an encounter is rare.

Creatures of the cane

The small furry beast with a bushy tail that darts across roads and into the bushes is not a

hings

squirrel or a rat, but a **mongoose.** Introduced from India in the late 19th century, these creatures were brought in to cull rats and poisonous snakes that thrived in the cane fields. Having no natural predators, they have reproduced unchecked and are today found all over the island in both the towns and countryside.

A secret weapon used in the sugar industry was the toad (*bufo marinus*), commonly referred to as the **cane toad** or *crapaud*. First introduced in 1835, it was brought in to control widespread insect damage to the cane crop. These toads are found in large numbers throughout the island and they can often be seen puddle-jumping across the road during the rainy season. They are capable of emitting a mild toxin and therefore should not be handled.

At one time even the **camel** was brought to Barbados to work as a pack animal in the cane fields;

Below: A morning stroll for three noble steeds. Right: The brown pelican was once seen throughout the island, but today they reside only at the Barbados Wildlife Reserve.

however its stay was short-lived.

Coastal critters
If you are staying at a beach house, the chances are you will share your lot with **land crabs**. Living in underground burrows, these creatures venture forth at night to forage for food. Often their eyes can be seen protruding from the entrance to their lair as they wait for the coast to clear (literally!). Some

species grow to a decent size and are considered a local delicacy. Smaller species can be seen on most beaches throughout the day, scuttling to and from their burrows.

You may be fortunate enough to see one of Barbados' rare but beautiful sights – a nesting **turtle.** West coast beaches are used by hawksbills and east coast beaches by leatherbacks. Guided by a genetically implanted homing instinct, they return to lay their eggs on the very beach on which they were born. Using their flippers, they dig a hole in the sand, deposit their eggs, and then carefully cover them completely with sand before lumbering back to the sea. This process takes a little over an hour and can be quietly viewed from a distance of a few feet – turtles seem oblivious to their human audience once egg-laying has started. Occurring only at night and typically between the months of April and October, the 150 or so eggs laid in each nest have a gestation period of about sixty days. It will then be some fifty years before a hatchling is ready to return to lay her own eggs. More information on turtles is available from the Belairs Research Institute in Holetown (Tel: 422-2087). Turtles are an endangered species and any sightings of nests, nesting activities, or hatchlings should be reported to the institute's '*Turtle Hotline*' on Tel: 230-0142.

Back on land

The island has an indigenous population of approximately 14,000 **green monkeys** (*cercopithecus sabaeus*), which was introduced from Africa over three centuries ago. The species, which provides some eighty per cent of the world's polio vaccine, is most commonly seen in the **Barbados Wildlife Reserve** in St. Peter. This is run by the Barbados Primate Research Centre and is also home to a variety of other fauna, including **brocket deer, agouti, hare,** and the **West Indian tortoise** – as well as numerous reptiles. There is also an aviary with abundant bird life. (See *Sightseeing Spectacular, page 38*).

Left: Iguana in the Barbados Wildlife Reserve.

Although now domesticated, the **black-bellied sheep** deserves mention as it is another unique Barbadian species. Reared here since the early days of colonisation and bred for its meat, it was originally a cross between an African hair sheep and a European wool sheep.

As the mongoose has put paid to the poisonous snakes on the island, there is really only one 'wild creature' to be avoided. Easily distinguished because of its segmented body and well-defined pairs of legs, it is the **centipede.** Brown or reddish in colour, it can grow to 6 or 8 inches (15 or 20 cm) in length, and its poisonous bite can put you in bed. Fortunately, they are not common and favour habitats such as derelict buildings, piles of dead leaves, and the like.

Bird life

Graeme Hall Bird Sanctuary on the island's south coast is one of the few remaining mangrove swamps on the island, and covers more than 90 acres (36 hectares). Formerly known as Graeme Hall Swamp, it was rescued from a slow, but almost certain demise in the mid-1990s when an agreement was negotiated between the private sector and government. Over 150 species of migratory birds have been recorded in Barbados, a significant number of which stop at the sanctuary *en route* to South America.

Common visitors include **warblers, waders, harriers,** and **falcons;** the **yellow-crowned night heron** and the **eskimo curlew** are rarer. The last recorded sighting of the latter in

Barbados was made in 1963. There are some forty species of resident birds on the island, almost half of which can be found at Graeme Hall. These include the **green heron**, the **moorhen,** the **yellow warbler** and three species of **egret.** Two walk-in aviaries house birds from the Caribbean and South America, while the large lake at the centre of the swamp provide a habitat for forty or so species of fish, such as **tarpon**, **mullet,** and **snook.**

Other native birds likely to be encountered include the **hummingbird**, **bananquit, blackbird, dove** and **cowbird.**

Above: Green heron at the Graeme Hall Bird Sanctuary. Below: Shy brocket deer at the Barbados Wildlife Reserve.

a place

Like most of the island's cultural heritage, Barbados' architecture is the product of many influences. Classical styles combined with the whim of local artisans, and the peculiarities of the tropical climate have given rise to some unique buildings and ingenious adaptatations. But to get to the root of how it all evolved, one must turn the clock back a bit.

Available materials

In the early days, Barbados was, for the most part, covered in dense tropical forest. The advent of the sugar industry in the mid-17th century led to vast areas of land being cleared for cultivation. The felled timbers provided the raw materials for the island's earliest buildings. Stick-and-brush shelters gave way to wattle-and-daub (branches and twigs plastered over with mud), which were thatched with long grasses, sugar cane, or palm fronds. "Lemonade walls" were built with a mortar of lime, molasses, and water.

Coral stone came next. Quarried from all over the island, it was a far superior building material that – unlike its forest predecessors – would not run out. The "Slave Huts", as they became known,

o live

were low thick-walled buildings made from coral with a thatched "hip– roof" one that slopes down on all four sides.

Although its *raison d'être* is somewhat hazy, the next building to appear was the classic – and wholly Barbadian – 'Chattel House'. Chattel means moveable property, and since many people did not own the land on which they lived following Emancipation, it is assumed that these houses were built with mobility in mind. No foundations were dug; instead the house rested on piles of loose rocks or coral blocks. A modular construction ensured that houses could be taken apart, moved, and put back together again in their new location.

The basic unit was rectangular, with a wooden frame covered

with pine boards or siding. The roof was steeply gabled, or hipped, and typically made from galvanised sheeting, often with fretted barge boards added at the gable ends. Wooden tiles known as shingles were sometimes used on the roof and walls.

The front of the house contained a central door (often glazed and shuttered) with a window on either side. These windows were usually hooded to keep out the rain, and many were complimented by slatted wooden shutters, known as "jalousies". Even when closed, a cool breeze could still move about the house. A porch was

often added with delicately-carved fretwork and turned wooden posts.

Such was the traditional Bajan chattel. This basic unit could be added to in kind, with a second or third appearing behind the first. The last would traditionally be a flat-roofed shed, hence the term "shed roof". Other additions included verandas, front galleries (the local term applied to a covered veranda), and in some cases a second storey. It is thought that the design of the veranda originated in India and was brought to the island by British settlers.

Far left: The Gothic St. John's Parish church looks over miles of jagged coastline. Its arched windows and doors were first built in the mid-17th century. Centre: An example of the original "Slave Hut" in Tyrol Cot Heritage Village. Top: Brightly-painted example of a chattel house.

A few chattel houses are still built in the traditional way, but most now draw only on the elements of style and have eliminated the original concept of mobility. Some are built on a solid base of concrete blocks and others atop a ground floor of stone. The recently-completed **Chattel House Village** in Sunset Crest, near Holetown, is a tribute to the longevity and popularity of this charming design.

The Great Houses

Meanwhile, the planters were busying themselves with the construction of their own houses, not surprisingly known as "Plantation Houses" or "Great Houses". Their size and design varied enormously, from the small simple houses such as **The Garden** in St. Lucy – birthplace of the late Prime Minister Errol Walton Barrow – to such Jacobean splendours as **St. Nicholas Abbey** and **Drax Hall**.

The traditional planter's house was a low, thick-walled building

Top: The elegant Francia Plantation was built at the turn of the twentieth century. Its double-jalousied windows are rare in Barbados. Centre: The walls of Sunbury Plantation House are original and were built from coral blocks and ballast from British ships. Bottom: St. Nicholas Abbey, built in the 1650s, is the oldest house on Barbados and features distinctive gables.

with a hip roof and tray ceilings. It had a cellar below ground level to store produce, and a second storey that made up the living quarters. The main entrance incorporated a double staircase – a Palladian style used extensively in Barbados. Examples of this design include **Sunbury Plantation House** in St. Philip, **Indian Pond** in St. Joseph, and **Lancaster** in St. James.

Many of the larger plantation houses that exist today were originally built to this same plan, but were extended as sugar profits and families grew. Verandas of wood or stone were added, as were extra wings and, in some cases, a third storey. A stone parapet to protect the roof from strong winds was another common addition. The influence of Georgian architecture in Barbadian plantation houses is apparent and features like arcaded stone porches and porticos, quoins at the corners of the building and around the windows, are common.

Building for the city

The island's urban architecture is also worthy of mention. The first buildings in Bridgetown were constructed from timber, and records indicate that almost almost eighty per cent of these were destroyed in a terrible fire in

1688. Trade with the Dutch was at a peak, and the rebuilt city demonstrated a marked Dutch influence – most notably in the proliferation of curved, gabled roofs. Few of these were to survive. Bridgetown suffered many more fires, including an inferno in 1766 that engulfed some 26 acres (10 hectares) of the city and destroyed almost 1,200 buildings. As a result, Parliament decreed that all new buildings were to be made of stone, a ruling that was to have a major impact on the city's development. The last major fire burned in 1860, taking some 10 acres (4 hectares) of the city with it. Consequently there are few buildings in Bridgetown that pre-date this period.

The city contains an eclectic mix of styles. Old bonded warehouses are found on either side of the Careenage, some complete with the original cast-iron davits used for loading cargo.

The **Parliament** buildings in the centre of town are a fine example of neo-Gothic architecture, while at the other end of Broad Street lies the imposing **Mutual Building** (built 1894–5) with its square turrets, silver domes, and ornate Victorian cast-iron balconies. The old **DaCostas** warehouse on Wharf Road is a Georgian classic, and on the corner of James and Lucas streets lies **Harford Chambers**, the city's oldest building. It has one of the few remaining curved Dutch gables. Roebuck Street and Baxters Road contain many of the island's old "shop houses": the ground floor was the shop premise and the top floor the merchant's living quarters. A wooden balcony or gallery, often supported by carved wooden posts, jutted out over the street.

Outside the city the residential neighbourhoods of Cheapside, Fontabelle, and Belmont Road all contain classic Bajan suburban houses. Most were built from stone, some from wood, but typical features included Palladian staircases, covered verandas (referred to locally as a galleries), jalousied windows, recessed masonary panels, hip roofs, and stone parapets. The curved parapet evident throughout the

Left: Tiny roadside chattel house near to Holetown. Below: The Garrison area is full of superb examples of Georgian architecture. The Main Guard built in 1803, with its red tower and bright green cupola, was the original guardhouse.

Above: Tiny wooden houses with jalousied windows and corrugated iron roofs are found throughout the island. Opposite: One of four lighthouses left on Barbados.

island is another wholly Barbadian peculiarity that first appeared in the middle of the 19th century.

No mention of urban architecture would be complete without a look at Speightstown, the island's second-largest town, in the northern parish of St. Peter. At the height of the sugar industry it was a thriving seaport, and was referred to as "Little Bristol" due to the busy trade with this English port. Speightstown has never benefited substantially from tourism and has changed little since the decline of the sugar industry.

The town retains much of its original character and charm, and has a distinctly "Olde Worlde"

feeling. Church Street has a row of charming old shop houses on one side, and the recently-restored parish church on the other. The post office and library building on Queen Street is pure Georgian; its otherwise austere facade brightened by the addition of window pelmets and a single staircase and gallery. This latter feature, similar to half a Palladian staircase, was quite common in Speightstown and can be found on several of the older buildings.

The three-storey building on Queen Street now occupied by pharmacist Noel Roach and Sons is built from bricks that arrived as ballast on a Bristol schooner. The walls are over two feet (half a metre) thick, while the third-floor dormer windows bear the unmistakable influence of the chattel house – corrugated iron

roofs, jalousied windows, and wooden shingles. It features a first floor verandah on the front face of the building. **Arlington Hall** is one of the oldest of the town's buildings. Tall, thin, and steeply gabled, it is typical of the very early townhouses found in Bridgetown. Essentially a medieval-style house, it is one-room wide and tapers toward the rear, with a business premise on the ground floor. It has a separate stair hall built at right angles to the main house and a grand staircase fronted by tall wrought-iron gates that enter at first-floor level from the street.

Forts and churches

Both war and religion have their places in the island's architectural heritage. In the 17th century, fortifications were built that ran the entire length of the south and west coasts the best-preserved example being **Charles Fort** (originally called Needham's Fort), located in the grounds of the Hilton Hotel. A chain of six signal stations was established between 1818–19, believed to have been originally intended for internal security following the slave rebellion of 1816. **Gun Hill** in St. George, **Cotton Tower** in St. Joseph, and **Grenade Hall** in St. Peter have all been restored and are open to the public. The extensive buildings of the **Garrison** complex just south of Bridgetown were the headquarters of the British Expeditionary Forces during the early 19th century. Most are well preserved and have attracted tenants, such as the Barbados Museum and Historical Society.

There are more churches in Barbados than days of the year, and true to form they come in all shapes and sizes. Small wooden "chattel-churches" are found throughout the island, while stately Anglican churches preside over each parish. Bridgetown is home to both a synagogue and a mosque, as well as Roman Catholic and Anglican cathedrals. Crenellated battlements; vaulted ceilings; clock towers; bull's-eye, triangular, and lancet windows; Byzantine-style belfries, and ornate pinnacles are some of the many features that appear on Barbadian churches.

St. Andrew's Parish Church has the distinction of being the only church not to have been destroyed by a hurricane, and **St. Patrick's Roman Catholic Cathedral** is a neo-Gothic marvel with stained glass windows that pivot to let in the breeze a truly Caribbean adaptation.

In a class of their own

Inevitably there are many buildings that do not fall within any one category, but still have particular architectural significance. One of these is the **Morgan Lewis Mill** in St. Andrew, the only windmill in the Caribbean that has survived with all its machinery intact. One of a fleet of over 500 that once ground cane in Barbados, its sails last turned in 1947. The island also has four lighthouses including the unique **South Point lighthouse**, constructed entirely of iron. Built in 1852, it is one of only a handful that remain world wide. Finally, the beautiful Regency mansion of **Sam Lord's Castle** in St. Philip is well worth a visit. Double verandas and staircases are present on all four sides; and the decorative plaster ceilings were built by Charles Rutter, whose work can be seen on the ceilings of Windsor Castle in England.

Many of the island's historic buildings have not survived. Neglected and left to decay, they have vanished, taking with them an irreplacable door to the past. However, recent years have seen an upsurge in the preservation and restoration of older buildings by both private and public

sectors. Even modern vernacular architecture seems sympathetic (with a few notable exceptions), and many features from the past are echoed in new buildings. Barbados's architectural heritage is alive and well, and if present trends and prevail, it will continue to thrive.

festivals

spectacular carnival parade through the packed streets of Bridgetown. Crop Over starts in July with the symbolic delivery of the last canes heralding the end of the sugar cane harvest. This sparks a series of events featuring variety shows; special Crop Over fairs; a Bajan culture village; a decorated cart parade; a Kadooment for children and, of course, the prestigious calypso competition, which eventually produces the 'Calypso Monarch' for the year.

Calypso is an integral part of the Crop Over celebration, and its Afro-Spanish rhythms are as important to the festival as is the sugar itself. It is the lyrics that make calypso so intriguing, as they spare no blushes and pack plenty of social bite. Politicians and events of the day bear the brunt of most compositions, which come fast and furious. Judging eventually eliminates all but the very best, and the grand finale is the 'Pic-O-de-Crop' show at which the Calypso Monarch is revealed and crowned.

Bajans love to féte, which is abundantly evident from the existence of the many festivals held on the island during the year. Until 1997, the major annual festivals were dubbed 'The Magnificent Seven', but new events and celebrations has extended the programme to encompass nearly every month.

Bringing in the harvest
The island's major festival is the traditional celebration of the harvesting of the sugar crop. 'King Sugar' may have lost some of its sweetness in the economy, but the **Crop Over Festival** remains the premier cultural event in the Bajan tourism calendar and attracts revellers from all over the world every July and August.

Crop Over is much more than a carnival and is not solely confined to the razzmatazz associated with its music, dance and partying. It embraces the island's heritage and the series of craft exhibitions, community games and fairs held during Crop Over highlight the impact that the sugar cane harvest has had on the economy for over 300 years.

However, Crop Over for most people is the cultural backcloth for a magnificent celebration of music and dance, culminating with **Kadooment Day** on the first Monday in August – the biggest party of the year. *Kadooment* is Bajan slang for 'fuss' or 'important event' and it certainly lives up to its billing, with a

and events

A *cohobblopot* is a grand 'cook-up' in Bajan slang, with all the ingredients mixed in the same pot. It is also the name of the final event prior to Kadooment, when the National Stadium is buzzing with the presence of the Calypso Monarch, the King and Queen of Costume Bands, and the Junior Monarch.

The Cohobblopot is an exciting mix of drama, dance, and a wide variety of music embracing calypso, tuk band, steel pan, reggae, folk, and gospel. The next morning many of the late-night revellers return to the National Stadium, dressed in colourful costumes to dance their way to Spring Garden Highway through crowded streets of well-wishers. The parade finishes close to Brighton Beach, but the party continues long and late.

Visitors are welcome to participate. Telephone the National Cultural Foundation on 424-0907 for further information. If you simply want to watch, there are plenty of good spots, but get there early and take a seat with you – the parade lasts for over four hours!

The **Holetown Festival** in St James is another community-based celebration, and takes its theme from the 17 February anniversary of the first English settlers arriving in Barbados. St James Parish Church is a focal point for the church activities, with medieval hymns being sung. Old folk songs are sung at other events, which also feature dancing, parades, street games, market stalls and exhibitions.

In 1993 John and Wendy Kidd established the **Holder's Season** as a unique Caribbean celebration of opera, music, theatre, and sport. Set in their beautiful grounds at Holder's Hill, the April festival has captured the cultural imagination of an international audience and won widespread acclaim for its ingenuity.

In 1997, the world-renowned opera tenor Luciano Pavarotti brought the curtain down on the season. To a packed gathering on the Holder's Hill polo field, the great Italian captivated his audience with his sensational and masterful performance.

The London Philarmonic Orchestra and the Desperados Steel Orchestra from Trinidad have also given stirring performances. Another feature of the 1997 Holder's Season was the production of the 18th-century Barbadian musical *Inkle and Yarico*. Last performed in 1830, the opera was an unparalleled success and became the platform for the creation of the Holder's Band, as well as the production of a contemporary *Inkle and Yarico* cabaret show, and subsequent performances in North America and England.

Left and below: Revellers wearing dazzling costumes dance through the streets during the Kadooment Day celebrations.

The Season also features a sporting element, with an annual cricket match at Holder's Green and a golf tournament at the prestigious Royal Westmoreland.

For more information contact John Kidd at the Holder's Season Box Office, telephone: 432-6385 or fax: 432-6461.

The Barbados festival season starts in January with '**Paint it Jazz**'. The island has a great tradition for jazz and has produced some excellent musicians such as Arturo Tappin and Andre Woodvine. The week-long festival attracts top-class international artists; among those who have performed in the past are Roberta Flack, Pattie La Belle, Al Jarreau, the Havana Ensemble, and Ray Charles.

The **Oistins Fish Festival** pays tribute to the island's fishing community, which is largely centred in the area. The Fish Festival has also played an important part in promoting the village and its local fishermen. Staged over the Easter weekend, there are competitions in fishing, fish-boning, net throwing, boat races, crab racing, sandcastle building, fish skinning, tray racing and cricket. The festival begins with the ceremonial blowing of

conch shells, which were used in the old days to let the villagers know that the fishing boats had safely returned to harbour with their daily catch.

From Easter Saturday to Easter Monday, the Oistins festival is one large street fair and another opportunity for Bajans and visitors to 'jump up' to vibrant Caribbean music or simply 'lime' with a few beers and some fish fry. It is also a good opportunity for the locals to sell their crafts at the many street stalls. The music at the festival embraces calypso, tuk band, steel pan, gospel, and drama, and there is also an exhibition by the Barbados Landship.

The finale of the Oistins Fish Festival takes place on Easter Monday, when the main event is the fish-boning competition with the coveted title of Fish-Boning Queen to be won.

The **National Independence Festival of Creative Arts** commemorates the day in 1966 when Barbados became independent. The celebration focuses on a wide variety of competitions, culminating in the grand finale on 30 November, which is **Independence Day** and also a national holiday. The

competitions include music, dance, singing, acting, writing, photography, art, and craft.

Independence Day celebrations are enthusiastically embraced by the whole community. A formal ceremony is held early in the morning at the historic Garrison, and this gives visitors an excellent opportunity to watch all the pomp and pageantry of a proud young nation.

The Multi-National Women's Group hosts an **International Festival and Fair** at Government House in early February. This cultural event includes performances by local artists and highlights Bajan arts and crafts, food products and cuisine. It is a worthy cause as the proceeds go to the betterment of life for young people in Barbados.

The **Congaline Festival** held in late April is a nine-day event that is actually a big street party. It culminates in a huge one-day 'T-shirt band' parade that weaves its way to Bridgetown like a long, colourful snake.

Barbados is a very religious island and music forms a big part of spiritual expression. It is against this background that **Gospelfest** was established in 1993. It has since grown to be a traditional

Whitsun festival for Christian communities at home and abroad. The three-day spiritual celebration is a family event that attracts both local and international performers.

During the last two weeks in May, the **Celtic Festival** celebrates the contribution that people with Celtic origins have made to the development of the Caribbean. Visiting choirs, musicians, and dancers from Europe combine to provide an entertaining programme of events featuring Gaelic song and dance. Many of the events are performed at schools and in community halls, while 'theme' ale-houses like McBrides, Shenanigans, and the Carib Beach Bar are the focal points for entertainment.

Sporting festivals are prominent throughout the year (*see 'A Sporting Life', page 112*). The most popular sport is cricket and the biggest event is the visit of the touring test team in March and April. Everything stops during a test match in Barbados!

The **Fred Rumsey Festival** in November features many visiting cricketers and celebrities from England, who join with the locals for two weeks of festival cricket, and some hearty socialising.

Horse-racing has its biggest festival in March with the running of the prestigious **Sandy Lane Gold Cup** – the biggest race in the Caribbean. All visitors are welcome at this race track, which is like a Caribbean Royal Ascot on Gold Cup Day.

Hockey has its **Banks Beer International Hockey Festival** in late August, when teams from all over the world compete with the locals on and off the field in a series of sporting and social events packed with fun, games and enjoyment.

The **Mount Gay/Boatyard Barbados International Regatta** over Whitsun in May features three days of racing, a plethora of watersports activities, and a vibrant social itinerary to close the competitive Caribbean regatta season.

In motorsport the **Barbados Texaco Havoline International Rally** in May is an exciting forty-eight hour event over some of the most demanding terrain in the Caribbean.

The **National Surfing Championships** are held in November in Bathsheba, while the '**Run Barbados**' road race series in December attracts many top marathon runners.

FESTIVAL & EVENTS SUMMARY

January	Paint it Jazz (tel: 429 2084)
February	Holetown Festival (tel: 430 7300) Multinational Women's Group International Festival
March	Test Cricket (tel: 426 5128) Sandy Lane Gold Cup Day
April	Oistins Festival (tel: 428 6738) Holder's Season (tel: 432-6385) Congaline Festival (tel: 424 0909)
May	Gospelfest (tel: 430 7300) Celtic Festival (tel: 430 7300) Barbados Texaco Havoline International Rally Mount Gay/Boatyard Barbados International Regatta
July	Crop Over Festival (tel: 424 0907)
August	Kadooment Day (tel: 424 0907) Banks International Hockey Festival
October	National Independence Festival of the Creative Arts (tel: 424 0909)
November	Independence celebrations Fred Rumsey Cricket Festival National Surfing Championships
December	'Run Barbados' Road Race Series

culture

club

Over the last three hundred years, British, African and other influences have given Barbados an unusual and captivating legacy of architecture, cuisine, dance, music, theatre, craft and art. This rich and diverse cultural heritage has given this jewel of an island its own unquestionably unique character. Disproportionate to its size, Barbados has produced a phenomenal array of scholars, artists, musicians, sportsmen and professionals, many of whom have contributed their talents to the rest of the world.

The people of Barbados are, by both nature and necessity, productive, talented, creative, self-disciplined, intelligent, confident, proud and happy. And as Barbados moves into the twenty-first century, today's Bajan can look back upon the efforts of his or her forefathers and draw great confidence from their efforts.

Bajan folklore and beliefs

Many Bajan folk beliefs and customs which survive in the oral tradition date back to the island's African heritage and even today many persist in a diluted form. (*See The Barbados Experience page 27*).

Bajan dialect and proverbs

A fusion of African and European speech, the lilting Bajan dialect has a rich and unique vocabulary: a consistent feature being that Bajans use the present tense of a verb even when speaking about past action.

Similarly, proverbs embodying folk values and words of wisdom are used in conversation. Expressed with a lyrical jingle, they capture the cadence and melody of Bajan speech. Shrewd and often witty, one such pearl is the saying: "*Goat head every day better dan cow head every Sunday*", meaning: "It is better to be given reasonably good treatment all the time than first-class treatment occasionally".

Calypso Rules!

When the sun sets on the Caribbean horizon, Barbados explodes into a colourful display of music so intense that the island is considered one of the entertainment centres of the Eastern Caribbean. It is a justly-deserved reputation. Steel bands and, to a greater extent, reggae enjoy popularity among the islanders, but it is calypso with its infectious, up-tempo rhythms and Bajan lyrics that endures as the musical identity of Barbados.

Its origins are in the slave songs brought by Africans to the West Indies in the early 1600s. They brought two distinct types of music – work songs and ribald songs. The work songs were sung to lift the spirit and were usually laments on the hardships they suffered. The lighter, satirical songs were like the social commentaries that are characteristic of today's calypso.

The primary form of resistance to cultural pressures at the time was the music of the "tuk" band, which still survives today. The name comes from the sound –"Boom-a-tuk, boom-a-tuk" – that the large log drum gives out. The music is lively, with an intricate, pulsating, quick beat strongly suggestive of British military bands. The regimental rhythms are superimposed on a persistent and recognisable African base. The result is a seductive, semi-martial rhythm that excites even the most staid villages to dance or "work up" as Bajans would say. Tuk bands travel from village to village

Top left: Souvenir dolls characterize the colour of traditional music and dance in Barbados. Top right: Jill Walker's captivating paintings portray a vivid side of life in Barbados. Left: Barbados dance traditions are a swirl of colour and light. Right: Hand-painted pottery by Juliana decorated in rich kaleidoscopic shades.

playing popular tunes and inviting villagers to contribute their own compositions as long as they fit the lively tempo. People dress up as donkeys or bears and dance in a suggestive manner. The melodies of tuk songs are simple and the subjects are trivial.

Above: The psychedelic colours of the Caribbean are captured here in a painting at the art studio in Perseverance. Right: The culture of Barbados is rich with arts and crafts. Opposite: From the earliest times dance in Barbados has been imbued with a deep passion and energy.

For centuries, church and state tried to ban this African-inspired music, but its sheer energy proved inextinguishable. Since the early 20th century, Barbadian music has been influenced and enhanced by the melodies of neighbouring Trinidad. The choral tradition which helped to keep the early Bajans spiritually buoyant has since emerged as contemporary calypso.

Interestingly, the lyrical themes of these songs have widened beyond the realm of gossip and scandal to include satire and social commentary. The sound of the words are as important as the words themselves, with double meanings, expressive folk sayings and stories told with great gesturing and emotion.

Due in part to the prevailing convention of the British, the singing of calypso was deemed by Bajan society to be incompatible with achieving positive social status and prestige. Early calypsonians were perceived as wandering buskers, jokers and comics rather than as serious singers. Yet those calypso pioneers persisted, encouraged both by conviction and the necessity to earn a living.

Calypso is heard everywhere: on the radio and in nightclubs and hotels. Calypsonians offer a wide range of perspectives on social issues, keeping the public informed and entertained. Topical and seductive, this music is – as The Mighty Gabby, the island's undisputed King of Calypso proclaims – an integral part of the island's culture.

There is always plenty of live entertainment on the hotel and club circuits. Employing some of the island's finest musicians and bands, venues such as **The Ship Inn**, **The Boat Yard**, **The Coach House** and **Harbour Lights** offer visitors the opportunity to see celebrated musicians.

The atmosphere at the clubs is always relaxed, so the bands are able to play with vigour, extravagance and abandon. A highly memorable, exciting evening is virtually guaranteed.

Dance and Theatre

In Barbados, one has only to take a leisurely stroll down any busy street to realise that everyday life here is high theatre. Music and dance is everywhere: at parties, in church and on mini-buses. Portable radios bring calypso to the streets day and night. It is claimed that Barbadian children begin to dance before they can walk! From this passion comes performing arts infused with spontaneity and energy and there is far more to the island's culture than flaming limbo and a poolside steel band. The many local dance performances, concerts and annual festivals are spectacles revealing the heart of Bajan culture.

From earliest times, there were two dance traditions on Barbados: the more formalised European dances of the planters, and the spontaneous dances of the slaves, rooted in West African tradition. Although the plantation owners tried to prohibit slaves from gathering to play music and dance fearing a prelude to rebellion, they soon realised that allowing the slaves to enjoy their own form of dance and music encouraged greater productivity and content.

The West African tradition of pelvic gyration, still seen in West Indian dance, both fascinated and horrified early white witnesses, who described this African-inspired dance as "indecent, wanton and lascivious". Bajans call it "wukin", and is frequently seen as tuk bands joyously parade through the streets.

Modern dance on Barbados which is abstract and expressionistic, began as a rejection of formalism and sterility. It was introduced to the island in 1968 by Mary Stevens, founder of the **Barbados Dance Theatre Company**. This dance group seeks to develop a greater interest among young people in cultural affairs and to promote community spirit through dance.

Performances by the Barbados Dance Theatre Company's remain indelibly etched in the memories of their audience. They successfully combine native folk tales and modern dance techniques to produce a medium that is intrinsically West Indian.

Similarly, the **Tryona Contemporary Theatre**, a group of dancers and musicians who perform at many of the island's hotels, believe the artist should be inspired to reflect his or her society by studying the way Bajans walk, act and gesticulate.

At the **Plantation Restaurant and Garden Theatre** in Christ Church, the *Tropical Spectacular* dinner show is a fantastic evening of entertainment. Retaining the magical formula that has made this show an astounding success for the past thirteen years, its' producers have successfully created an authentically Caribbean, cultural extravaganza with fabulous costumes and exhilarating choreography.

An exotic display of rich music and dance, the show combines the agile versatility of the Plantation Dancers, the red-hot exploits of fire-eater Cassius Clay and all the excitement of expertly-performed fire limbo.

The evening contains all the ingredients that have worked on visitors and locals alike, who return time and time again, thus earning the show an unrivalled reputation as a "must-see" experience that is excellent value for money.

Complimentary transport whisks visitors to dance the night away to the pounding beat of the steel band and the potent, electrifying sounds of Spice & Company. The buffet dinner is one of the best on the island and includes unlimited free drinks.

This unique production spans time from pre-historic to the present, capturing artistic expressions that have emerged from the Caribbean's rich melting pot. It begins, fittingly, with a tribute to Barbados' first inhabitants, the peaceful Arawaks, before moving back yet

Photographs: A brilliant spectacle of colour and light, the Tropical Spectacular *at the Plantation Restaurant and Garden Theatre in Christ Church, is a fabulous evening's entertainment.*

further in time and faster in tempo for a stirring retrospective of the dazzling *Yoruba* dancers of West Africa.

The scene then shifts smoothly into the bygone festivities of Bridgetown market on a Saturday morning. Against a medley of traditional folk music and clothed in vivid creole costumes, characters like the coconut woman and the nutseller offer their wares and cast an enchanting spell to bring the curtain down on the first part of the show.

The second half of the show is a sensational journey through the kaleidoscopic celebrations and festivals of the Caribbean. Ablaze with colour and sound, and illuminated with skilful lighting effects, this cavalcade of cultures begins with the *Junkanoo* dancers of the Bahamas and includes a show-stopping sequence depicting a "zombie jamboree" of jumbies (spirits).

Back in Barbados, and in honour of the famous Crop Over festival, revelry is showcased in an explosion of exuberance that encompasses everything from the tuk band and masquerade folk characters like Shaggy Bear and Steel Donkey, to all the splendour of Kadooment. The show comes to a stunning climax as the entire cast jump-up bacchanal-style into a celebration of carnival in Trinidad.

Taking the stage

Theatre in Barbados began in the late 1600s with plantation improvisations known as "tea meetings", in which individuals recited passages, presented slapstick comedy routines and gave spontaneous speeches. Equally spontaneous were the *al fresco* performances given by newly-arrived troupes of actors who presented plays in the shadow of their ships.

The first mention of theatre in Barbados occurs in the diary of former US president George Washington. He noted, while on a trip to the island in 1751, (his one and only trip abroad), that he attended a presentation of *The Tragedy of George Barnwell*.

By 1783, a group called the **Patagonian Theatre** was presenting English plays, including performances of Shakespeare's works. However, they soon received swift competition from a rival called the **New Theatre**. Comedies and pantomimes drew audiences, but

these were exclusively for plantation-class whites. In fact, until the early 20th century, the smaller theatre groups in Barbados were exclusively white. However, after World War II the **Green Room Players** formed and began to stage productions of both local and international plays. Ranging from light farce to serious drama, the Green Room Players' efficiently-produced performances have entertained many generations of Barbadians and visitors. Among their popular comedies, playing to full-capacity crowds, are *Let's Go Bajan*, *Move Over Mrs Markham*, *Absurd Person Singular*, and *See How They Run*.

Stage One Theatre Productions, established in 1979, has carried on the tradition of producing works relevant to the Caribbean experience. The company's aim is to encourage greater interest and participation in theatre. One of Stage One's most successful productions was Errol John's *Moon on a Rainbow Shawl*, a play suffused with raw energy, set in a Caribbean backyard in the late 1940s. A more recently-estabalished island group, **Community Theatre Productions** was created to satisfy the demand for entertaining theatre

that utilises Barbadian material. The company wins consistent praise and their first event, an improvised folk comedy called *Laff It Off*, played to packed audiences at the Queen's Park Theatre. *Laff It Off* delighted Bajans and visitors alike with its amusing exploration of the wit and talent found within the everyday goings-on at a village

Below: The folk and dance culture of Barbados is displayed in many theatrical productions.

rum shop. Popular with locals, other productions such as *Pampalan,* which combines social and political comment in witty sketches and songs, have also found appreciation in Britain, Canada and the United States.

Weekend entertainment abounds in Barbados. In the villages, you will find Fridays and Saturdays are often filled with the sounds of music and laughter as residents enjoy a "village meet".

Most likely to tempt the visitor are the dinner shows which include live performances of traditional music and dance. Highly recommended, the show *1627 And All That*, originally produced by entrepreneur Andrew Nehaul, portrays the folk culture of Barbados.

Arts and Crafts

There are a number of art galleries in Barbados and each displays the diverse and imaginative work of some extraordinarily talented artists. Art is very personal and the best way to fully appreciate what is on offer is to visit the galleries.

The **Barbados Gallery of Art** in the historic Garrison area is dedicated exclusively to the visual arts. It collects, preserves, researches and exhibits 20th-century art from Barbados and boasts a permanent collection that includes artwork not only from the Caribbean, but also from neighbouring South America and the United States. Importantly, the Barbados Gallery of Art offers visitors the chance to view the best fine art from the nation. All exhibitions are temporary and rotate between four and six times a year. Exhibitions are organised from the permanent collection, and from other public and private sources.

The gallery was established in 1985 as the Art Collection Foundation and organised competitive exhibitions to form the nucleus of the gallery's permanent collection. In 1994, the foundation changed its name to

the Barbados Gallery of Art, and in October 1996 opened its doors to the public. The gallery's museum is home to some fascinating artefacts from old Barbados. On display are a number of picturesque old prints, maps, landscapes and colourful portrayals of the activities of an earlier era. The gallery is open from Tuesday to Saturday between 10am and 5pm. For further information telephone 228 0149.

Recently, Barbados has experienced a remarkable renaissance in cultural activity. The opening of the **Kirby Gallery** is one of the most vibrant examples of this exciting new era. Founded by Robert Kirby, a dedicated art collector, the gallery is pioneering in several ways, not only because of its significant size, but also in its determination to present specifically Barbados art in contrast to that of artists from the wider Caribbean.

Frequent exhibitions highlighting individual artists secure the gallery an always self-revitalising profile, as well as making the Kirby Gallery an important factor in the development and promotion of chosen artists.

Centrally located in Hastings, near the historic Garrison area, the Kirby Gallery enjoys the privilege of having its own premises in an old Barbadian residence, which was acquired and remodelled with the gallery in mind. (Telephone: 430-3032). Very conveniently, the gallery co-exists in this attractive location with the **Fast Frame Factory** which, with the expertise of its owner Shaka Rodney, has established itself as the largest company of its kind in Barbados.

Apart from a wide range of paintings, the gallery also sells prints and pottery. It is open from Monday to Friday between 10am and 7pm and on Saturday from 10pm to 2pm.

The **Verandah Gallery** on Broad Street sells local and Caribbean works and is within easy reach of busy downtown shoppers. They can even arrange to ship your purchase home.

The **Art Foundry** at Four Square is housed in an old coral stone building within the Heritage Park, the Art Foundry offers for sale an outstanding collection of

Far left: Unique shell art treasures make popular souvenirs. Left: Hand-crafted toy buses can be bought at the Potter's House next to Earthworks Pottery in Edghill. Above: The Kirby Gallery in Hastings features original works of art, limited edition prints and fine ceramics by local, regional and international artists.

paintings, sculpture, original prints, photographs, and fine crafts. Many Bajan artists portray scenes of everyday Caribbean life, while others delve into the world of the abstract.

Barbados has a rich heritage in cricket and many visitors are captivated by the paintings of well-known local artist David Skinner. His signed prints of such legendary cricket heroes as Sir

Above: The Earthworks Studio handcrafts and decorates a fascinating range of pottery. Right: Shoemaker in the Rastafarian Village at Temple Yard in Bridgetown. Far right: Brightly-painted crafts are sold at the Pelican Village.

Garfield Sobers and the fiery Wes Hall are particularly popular.

Conveniently, a number of hotels provide facilities for artists to either exhibit their work for a period of time or display pieces for sale on particular nights of the week. These travelling exhibitions often include craft work as well as paintings and drawings.

The African influence is still very prominent in the works of many Barbadian artists and craftsmen. The African heritage springs forth in the colours, themes and styles of many of Barbados' most creative citizens and is expressed in their own unique blend of art and craft.

The Barbadian artist will confound those who would make a distinction between art and craft. Taking simple, everyday items and skilfully working them into an expression of his or her personal and cultural self, the island's craftsmen have ornamented, embossed and embellished the functional, making it a work of art.

The Yard at the Quayside Centre stocks some wonderfully colourful Caribbean crafts, including some beautiful carved toys and animals, wall plaques, prints and copper jewellery.

Wild Feathers Bird Art is produced by Geoffrey and Joanie Skeet from their studio and home close to Sam Lord's Castle in St. Philip (Tel: 423-7758). Their primary work features carvings of the island's indigenous and migratory birds, but Joanie also paints watercolours of Caribbean birdlife which are reproduced on prints and notelets.

At **Temple Yard**, at the westerly end of Bridgetown, you can watch the Rastafarian craftsmen working with leather, straw, clay and wood. Listening to their joyous humming and the sounds of their mallets and chisels, you are instantly transported back to the Mother continent.

Here, at the **Rasta Craft Village**, the creations of a whole community of craftsmen are laid out: leather bags, shoes, purses as well as countless items created from wire, bamboo, coconut husks, shells and palm fronds. Images of local fish, birds, fruit and animals are sold, together with seashells clustered into fans and jewelled vases.

Pelican Village on Hincks Street is where the fashionable and the knowledgeable gather for shopping. Nearby is a massive, and rather contentious piece of *avant-garde* sculpture known as *Pelican In Flight*. It consists of three pylons welded together and soars above the crowds – albeit rusting in the sea breeze.

Another great place to buy crafts and souveniers is the **Women's Self-Help Co-operative** on Broad Street near the Nelson statue. It sells a wide variety of local goods, including pottery, crochet work, hand-made dolls, delicious local foods and cherry wine.

At various times of the year craft fairs are held to encourage the exposure of local talent. *(See Festivals, page 94 for further information).*

Shell art treasures are extremely popular with visitors, and Barbados has two exceptional sources for this work. A visit to **Daphne's Sea Shell Studio** is an unforgettable experience. The studio is located on Congo Road (Tel: 423-6180) at the back of an old plantation house. A new branch of the studio has opened next to the Kitchen Korner in Holetown. On entering, one is over-whelmed by a collage of Caribbean colours and an ocean of items to choose from.

Everything from fabulous shell mirrors, uniquely hand-crafted shell jewellery, Christmas ornaments, ceramics and frames and an outstanding line of hand-painted clothing and accessories can be found.

People visit Daphne's Shell Studio to capture the pure essence of its charm and creativity, as well as the warmth and hospitality of the family who work there.

The **Shell Gallery** is located at Carlton House in St. James (Tel: 422-2593). Founded by owner Maureen Edghill, it specialises in exotic shells from around the world. There is hand-painted chinaware from the exclusive *Seahorse and Fishmarket* collection, shell jewellery, local pottery, ceramics, batiks, and unique shell art. Maureen's work has won international awards and

she has been commissioned by the Barbados Museum for special works. There is not a luxury hotel or villa on the island that does not have at least one of her magnificent shell-decorated mirrors. On certain days, Maureen will take visitors around the workshop and demonstrate her intricate craft in person.

For pottery, visit the magnificent **Earthworks Studio** at Edghill Heights in St. Thomas run by Goldie Spieler and her son, David. Earthworks is the showcase for Bajan pottery and its origins date back to the mid 1970s when Goldie started the company in an endeavour to revive the craft. The company was the winner of the Barbados Industrial Development Corporation 1996 Quality Product Award. The capable staff handcraft and individually decorate a wide range of trinket boxes, dinnerware, vases, office and bathroom items, lamp bases, light covers and even custom-made tiles.

The designs reflect the blues, greens of the Caribbean sea and sky with occasional splashes of

Top: Hand-painted chairs and furniture are available the House of Art in Perseverance. Left: At Pelican Villiage on Harbour Street potters create interesting wares in their small studios.

yellow for the sunshine. Some works are specially commissioned for hotels, or as collector's items. Telephone 425-0223 for further information. All purchases can be packed and shipped worldwide. For many visitors, Earthworks becomes one of the unique memories of a wonderful holiday.

Next door is the blue-and-white **Potter's House** where one may wander and browse among carefully selected work that has been crafted to an exceptionally high standard. Unique items made from a ivariety of natural materials including wood, glass, metal, fabric, straw and, of course, clay are on sale. There is also a beautiful selection of hand-made local jewellery. The work of a number of Bajan artists are featured here. There is also a cosy café with a magnificent view where visitors can enjoy a cold drink and a tasty snack.

Barbados has a number of other excellent potteries, including **Red Clay Pottery and Fairfield Gallery** (Tel: 424-3800). They offer free tours and demonstrations and produce original designs. They are renowned for their large clay pots which are often found in the reception areas of some of the best hotels on the island.

There are plenty of shops that sell local art and hand-crafted souvenirs attached to the hotels on the St James coast and along Christ Church roads. They offer a wide range of batik and silk-screen dresses and printed fabrics, including wall-hangings and scarves. There are also a number of shops selling T-shirts, but few match the quality and designs of one local company, **Ganzee.** Their shops are scattered throughout the island, where their products are shown off in colourful displays.

At **Best of Barbados** gift shops, one can find the work of internationally acclaimed artist, Jill Walker. Her scenes and landscapes of the island hang on the walls of many Bridgetown offices, hotels, guesthouses and public places. Her representations of island life are delightfully ironic, and Jill is one of the most hardworking and popular artists in Barbados. With eight of her shops located around the island, visitors have easy access to a vast range of reasonably-priced goods, including posters, maps, cookbooks, tea towels, tiles, aprons and much more. Her paintings which appear on many souvenir items reflect the vibrant colours of the Caribbean.

Jill Walker has lived in the West Indies since 1955 when she married her husband, Jimmy who worked for the Barbadian government as an architect.

After their wedding, they spent three months travelling throughout the Caribbean islands during which time Jill developed a love for this part of the world. During the trip Jill painted and sold her work to boost their income and was offered various commissions in Antigua. Jimmy subsequently accepted an offer to work in Antigua and the couple spent three idyllic years on the island where Jill's artistic talents continued to develop. Her paintings started to include the traditional buildings and people of the West Indies for which she has since become so well known.

The Walkers returned to Barbados in 1960 and have lived there ever since. In the early 1970s they decided to form **Best of Barbados Ltd**. which has gone on to become the most successful chain of gift shops on the island. A family-run business, they offer an fine range of locally-made souvenirs.

Duty-free and local crafts are the two big 'shopping attractions' of Barbados. Some great duty-free deals can be found on jewellery, porcelain, and crystal. Barbados handicrafts are varied and are also duty-free. In general, shops are open from 8am–4pm Monday–Friday and 8am–12pm on Saturday. Few are open on Sundays.

Bajan shop assistants are friendly but come across as laid-back, so be patient at all times. Dress casually, but properly as Bajans do not welcome beachwear anywhere but on the beaches. Most shops accept major credit cards and traveller's cheques, while Barbados and US dollars are the accepted currency.

Remember, for duty-free shopping you will need your airline ticket and passport. For all duty-free purchases, you must leave a copy of any invoices with customs on departure from Barbados. Purchased goods can be taken at the time of purchase with the exception of liquor and tobacco, which will be delivered to your point of departure. The collection process is simple; staff will make the appropriate arrangements with the minimum of inconvenience.

The main shopping area in Barbados is Broad Street in Bridgetown. With its quaint colonial buildings and overhanging verandas this bustling through-fare has changed little over the past hundred years. In stark contrast are the modern department stores, well stocked with high-quality products and many duty-free bargains.

Both Grantley Adams Airport and the Port Terminal have duty-free shops, while others are scattered along the south and west coasts in small malls.

The **Chattel House Village**, **DaCostas West Mall**, and **Cave Shepherd** in Holetown, as well as a number of shopping plazas from Hastings to Oistins, offer a range of interesting shops.

The department stores are air-conditioned shops and stretch from Nelson's Monument at the Careenage to the Mutual Building on Lower Broad Street.

Jewellery

Jewellery features prominently in the aggressive marketing of leading duty-free retailers such as Diamonds International, Colombian Emeralds, Little Switzerland, The Royal Shop, Harrisons and Cave Shepherd.

A unique and reasonably-priced alternative to the above is **Luna Jewellers** on Bay Street, who design and make an innovative range of Barbadian jewellery inspired by the rich marine life of the Caribbean.

When it comes to department stores, **Cave Shepherd** leads the way. Visit the liquor and cigar store on the ground floor, which stocks a huge selection selection, at duty-free prices. **DaCostas Mall**, **Harrison's**, **Mall 34**, and the **Norman Centre** are the other popular malls, offering every conceivable merchandise – including local crafts. Steer clear of the imported items which are usually cheaper outside of Barbados and look instead for original local products.

Clothing

In the glamorous world of fashion, many shoppers will be attracted to the imaginative, innovative tropical designs. Barbados is associated with rich, vibrant colours and local designers have done much to capture a Caribbean flavour in their work.

Colours of the Caribbean next door to the Waterfront Café in the Careenage stocks a creative range of casual clothing and

you drop

accessories designed by owner Diane Butcher. **Upbeat** also offers a wide selection of top-quality Caribbean wear, while **Coconut Junction** and **Lazy Days** stock top brand names in swimwear.

Young Barbadian entrepreneurs Erica Weatherhead and Vicki Cozier have captured the imagination of the highly-competitive Bajan swimwear industry with an exclusive range of individually hand-painted products marketed under the 'Sandbox' label.

Fashionable boutiques are widespread in the main shopping centres and in the foyers of many of the leading hotels. **Gatsby** boutiques, in particular, are known for their quality clothing and accessories.

Books and music

Books are expensive in Barbados, although there is no substitute for the works of local writers. Some excellent books on Barbados and the Caribbean are available at leading bookstores like **Cloisters** in Hincks Street, **Days Books** at Speedbird House, **Bryden's** at Victoria Street, and on the second floor of Cave Shepherd. **Best of Barbados** which has branches around the island stocks a wide selection of

souvenir books on the island, as well as CDs and tapes of local musicians. Barbados has produced an amazing line of top-quality musicians like the legendary *Merrymen* who have been around for over thirty years. A blend of calypso, folk and modern, no trip to Barbados would be complete without a Merrymen souvenir.

Calypso, steel band and reggae also feature prominently; and island bands such as Square One, Krosfyah, Coalition, and For the People also produce some good modern disco and tropical sounds.

There is a record department on the ground floor of Cave Shepherd and the **Number One Record Store** in Bridgetown stock a good selection of local music.

Food

Locals mainly shop at the larger supermarkets which are found island-wide. Gas stations also have well-stocked convenience stores and fast-food facilities. Fresh fish, fruit, and vegetables are also sold from roadside stalls.

The most popular supermarkets on the south coast are **Big B** at the bottom of Rendezvous Ridge, **Super Centre** at Oistins, **Julie'N** at the Bussa roundabout, and **JB's**

at Sargeant's Village just off the highway. The west coast has a **Super Centre** at Sunset Crest, as well as **Jordan's** supermarkets at Fitt's Village and Speightstown. Elsewhere there are numerous convenience stores and mini-marts that cater to most needs.

Most foodstuffs can be purchased in Barbados, although imported goods are naturally more expensive. There is a large amount of imported fruit and vegetables which are expensive. Local fruit and vegetables may lack the overall lustre, but they offer better value for money. Meat is reasonably priced and is generally imported from the USA, Ireland and New Zealand.

Barbados bread is excellent, especially the top brands, *Purity* and *Zephirin*.

All supermarkets stock a wide range of soft drinks and alcohol. Rum is the cheapest of the spirits; wine is expensive but not outrageous. If you drink beer, then the local Banks beer is the best buy.

If you enjoy ice cream, then you will adore the local Bico brand. Made entirely from natural ingredients, it is world-class and provides delicious relief from the hot sun.

Cricket mania

Of all sports, cricket reigns supreme in Barbados. Bajans love cricket, with a passion that is much in evidence during test matches. The commercial hub of Barbados almost grinds to a halt when a test is being played at the hallowed Kensington Oval.

The gospel of cricket was spread by soldiers throughout the British Empire, but its roots in Barbados were to prove deeper and stronger than anywhere else. The soldiers billeted around the Garrison introduced the game to the locals, some of whom had played it while at boarding school

Bajans love their sport and go to great lengths to enjoy it. The healthy outdoor climate provides ideal conditions for most sports, although wisely, the more energetic activities avoid the midday sun.

Interestingly, it is Barbados' military ties that played a fundamental role in shaping the sporting culture of the island. It is said that in the late 18th century and early 19th century almost 20,000 soldiers died from disease in the Garrison area (on the outskirts of Bridgetown), which was once a swamp where vicious mosquitoes bred prolifically. However, by 1820 the Royal Engineers had laid the first of their drainage systems and, in addition to increasing the parade and drilling ground, it increased the area for other leisure activities.

Boredom was a big problem for the military command in those days, but the extended land around the barracks created new opportunities for additional activities – particularly cricket and horse-racing.

Today, the spacious suburban pasture of the Garrison Savannah is enclosed within the Barbados Turf Club's race track, and on most evenings an array of joggers can be seen weaving in all directions. The rugby pitch is a major part of the complex, while soccer, basket-ball, athletics and kite-flying are all popular.

This legacy of the old colonial days has stood the test of time and provides many Bajans with a sporting arena in which to enjoy their favourite activities.

ife

in England, and its popularity gradually spread to all corners of the island. The earliest known club was St Ann's, which was formed around 1805, but later disbanded.

In 1865 the first representative cricket match in the Caribbean took place when Barbados played and beat British Guyana. Although the headquarters of Barbados cricket moved to Bridgetown's Kensington Oval thirty years later, the game has continued to be played and enjoyed at the Garrison Savannah.

Pitches across the island vary from a cleared canefield to an empty stretch of beach, from a rural country setting to the resplendent Kensington Oval, arguably the most famous cricket ground in the Caribbean. Here the best of Barbados, the West Indies, and visiting touring teams have played the immortal game for over 100 years.

Some former cricketers lament at the apparent decline in the standard of the modern game and attribute the trend to the growing influx of other sports. American

Top left: Cricket is a game which arouses great passion amongst Bajans of all ages. Left: Soccer is a popular sport. Background: The verdant greens of the golf course at Sandy Lane.

CRICKET'S SPECIAL PLACE IN BARBADOS SOCIETY

Following its introduction into Bajan society around 1800, cricket became an integral part of everyday life in Barbados.

Bajans love their national game, and most have an opinion on every aspect of it. Matches are played everywhere across the island, and although the sport's early development was tainted by class and colour prejudice, this has long since disappeared. Overseas touring teams make visits to the island all year round, but the highlight of the busy season is the world renowned Kensington Oval test match.

The commercial life of Barbados almost grinds to a halt on test match days as many businesses close to allow their employees to attend. School children get a traditional holiday, and throughout the island transistor radios are strategically placed everywhere to record every incident and event.

Cricket in Barbados is not simply a passion; it is a religion. And in a sport where statistics are an integral part of its culture, many Bajans have left an indelible mark on its history.

At the top of this list are four exceptional cricketers, all knighted by Queen Elizabeth II for their very special service to the game. Sir Frank Worrell (1964) was one of the famous trio dubbed the 'Three Ws' in cricket folklore and the first black player to lead a West Indies team abroad. He was born to lead and had vision and statesmanship long before his time. But he was also an outstanding cricketer in his own right. At nineteen, he scored 308 not out against Trinidad in Bridgetown, adding 502 runs with John Goddard in just over six hours. Two years

later he teamed up with Clyde Walcott to score 574 runs in under six hours to establish another world record.

Sir Clyde Walcott (1994) was an outstanding athlete who became a much respected administrator and Chairman of the International Cricket Council. In the 574 runs record stand with Worrell in 1946 he scored 314 not out as a young twenty-year-old. At one stage in his career he hit twelve centuries in twelve consecutive test matches.

Sir Everton Weekes (1995) was a versatile fielder and an aggressive striker of the ball. An engaging sportsman, he once scored five successive test centuries before being controversially run out for 90 in Madras in 1948.

But for all-round brilliance, many cricket lovers throughout the world will view Sir Garfield 'Garry' Sobers as the greatest cricketer of all time. Knighted at the Garrison Savannah in 1976, he was the complete cricketer in every sense as a batsman, bowler, and outstanding fielder. He will always be remembered for his six sixes in an over off the hapless Malcolm Nash at Swansea in 1968 and for his world batting record of 365 not out at Sabina Park in Jamaica in 1957. He was gifted enough to also play soccer, golf and basketball for Barbados.

But while the four cricketing knights will always hold a special place in the anals of cricket history, there are many other household names in Barbados who have carved their niche in this greatest of all games. Others will continue to follow, inspired and enlightened by the feats of their illustrious predecessors.

television has given basketball a high profile, but other team sports like rugby, hockey, and netball have also widened their horizons.

Teams, tennis, and totes

Rugby continues to be centred at the Garrison and the traditional matches remain a feature of the annual fixture list. Tales of hard-fought matches with hard drinking to follow confirm a camaraderie and enjoyment that has long stood the test of time. The local fixture list continues to accomodate teams from visiting ships, touring teams, and matches within the Caribbean.

The highlight of a busy hockey season is the Banks Beer Hockey Festival in August. Sixty teams, many from overseas, take part in a packed programme of sporting and social events.

Tennis courts are widespread throughout the island and the game is thriving. Many hotels allow non-guests to hire courts when they are available. Squash and table tennis are also popular

and have the added benefit of usually being played in air-conditioned comfort.

By 1846, horse-racing was centred at the Garrison where many of the cavalry officers tested their horsemanship against the local gentry. Race days were highlights in the Bridgetown social calendar when the ladies dressed up in fine regalia and the military provided the pomp and pagentry to ensure a grand occasion. The perimeter of the track was bedecked with

Above: Tennis courts are part of the facilities offered by most top hotels throughout the island. Below: The 'Sport of Kings' has been a highlight in the Barbados social calendar for over a century.

carriages and colourfully-dressed spectators and with the music of the military band in the background, the races were keenly contested.

Dubbed the 'Sport of Kings', horse-racing still enjoys a healthy presence at the Garrison, with Gold Cup Day and Derby Day being the highlights. Corporate hospitality boxes and tote-betting are available, although many locals still prefer the hustle and bustle around the course.

In addition to horse-racing, there are several other equestrian sports. Polo at Holder's Hill started in 1965 – the sport having been brought to Barbados by the cavalry officers based at the Garrison in the last century. Teams from United States, Canada, England, and Argentina are the most frequent visitors to this lovely setting.

The elegant sport of dressage has grown in popularity since the mid-1990s, while show-jumping and cross-country events are two other disciplines gaining significant interest within a small but enthusiasic equestrian community.

Water sports

Inevitably it is the watersports which are mostly identified with the sporting life of a Caribbean island, and Barbados is no exception. Warm tropical breezes, clear turquoise waters, and pristine beaches are home to a plethora of water-sports including sunfish sailing, wind-surfing, swimming, kayaking and water-skiing.

Barbados is an island of varying coastlines, which allows each discipline to find its own favourite location. The tranquil beaches of the popular west coast contrasts dramatically with the pounding surf on the east coast, protected from the populous by a hilly terrain and winding rural roads. It is here that surfers feel most at home and where the famous 'Soup Bowl' plays host to the sport's elite competitors, both local and overseas.

Named because of its frothing surf appearance, the 'Soup Bowl' in Bathsheba is the perfect retreat for surfers. Most shoot the waves all day and then retire to the nearby Bonito Bar for a sundowner. Colourful surfboards propped against mini-mokes at sunset are testimony to a day well spent.

It is said that you can windsurf in Barbados all year round as both the west and south coasts offer excellent waves in the more popular locations. The serious windsurfers tend to prefer the windy south coast – Silver Sands in particular – while the Sandy Beach area, with its coral protected lagoon, is a popular and safe area for beginners. But the real experts see no boundaries in their quest for quality rides, and those who are prepared to move around the coastlines will be well rewarded for their efforts. Barbados's best-known windsurfer is Brian Talma, a colourful character who has been a wonderful ambassador for his sport and his homeland.

Above: Jet-skiing is popular from all beaches along the west and south coast.

Overseas visitors also include yachtsmen and, as the most easterly island in the Caribbean, Barbados has often been the first stop for many trans-Atlantic crossings. Sailing in almost ideal conditions has ensured a healthy survival for this sport. The internationally renowned Mount Gay Rum/Boatyard Barbados Regatta is dubbed the 'Fun Regatta' because of its vibrant social schedule and is the highlight of the Barbados yachting season. The three days of racing is the premier attraction in a packed programme of water-sports activities and closes with a grand féte and presentation ceremony at the Boatyard.

Game fishing is an exhilarating adventure in Barbados, and charter boats go to great lengths to ensure everyone enjoys this experience. The rewards can be enormous, judging by the 910-pound (410-kg) blue marlin that greets arrivals in the baggage hall of the Sir Grantley Adams Airport. Caught by Barbadian

enthusiast Graham Manning in 1996, it remains the largest single catch on rod and reel in the southern and eastern Caribbean. Tournaments are held throughout the year and boats can be chartered through the local association with membership, meals, and drinks inclusive.

Back on land

Motorsport and cycling make good use of excellent conditions with cyclists staging regular round-the-island races featuring some gruelling climbs in the more rural areas.

Bajans are car crazy and thus motorsports attracts a large following. The sport takes many forms, including rallying, racing, hill climbs, go-karting, auto sprints, and dirt-track racing.

With narrow winding roads set in beautiful countryside, it is easy to see why rallying is so popular in Barbados. Colourful participants – such as Richard 'Red Mout Ru' Roett, Peter 'Duct Tape' Thompson, and Trevor 'Electric Mouse' Manning, add extra zest to the competitions. The major event is the international All Stage Rally held in May which attracts overseas teams and forms an integral part of the Caribbean Rally Championship.

The quieter side of sport

Away from the furore and noise of motorsport, there are plenty of alternatives for those who prefer to be absorbed into the leisurely pace of Bajan life.

Above: The race-track in the Garrison area of Bridgetown. Left: Beachside cricket – part of the island's sporting heritage. Right: Children play the ancient game of Warri.

Golf is played at the Royal Westmoreland, Sandy Lane, and Rockley courses, and plans are afoot to build others to meet the seemingly insatiable demand of locals and visitors. The Royal Westmoreland course designed by Robert Trent-Jones is set amidst numerous fabulous villas, but Sandy Lane, with two eighteen-hole courses and one nine-hole course, will undoutedly become the focal point of golf in the region when the Sandy Lane Hotel, which is currently under total reconstruction, is opened in the year 2000.

For those who prefer to wander leisurely through the Bajan countryside, the National Trust organises Sunday morning rambles all-year round. Barbados has a rich heritage and, with a wide variety of walks, many of the island's natural and historic attractions can be visited. Visitors can also tour the island on horseback or mountain-bike with Highland Outdoor Tours, based in St Thomas. These tours take in local history, sugar cultivation, farming, flora, and fauna.

The ancient Egyptian board game of Warri continues to have a presence in the Speightstown area, but it has largely given way to dominoes in recent times. Bajans love to 'shoot a dom' and groups of players are often seen huddled under a coconut tree, outside a rum shop, or on a Bridgetown street corner. The added element of gambling makes these games fiercely competitive and often very noisy.

Bridge, chess, and draughts are also popular if less vociferous. Barbadians take great pride in their world draughts champion Ronald 'Suki' King – a master of the 'Go-As-You-Please' and 'Three-Move Restriction' disciplines.

There are few truly indigenous sports although 'road tennis' might qualify. A table tennis court is chalked out on the road and the game is played with a plank as the net. Crude wooden bats are essential equipment for a sport that originally developed in the rural areas but is now played island-wide.

Athletics has suffered due to a lack of facilities and limited competition, despite the best efforts of an enthusiastic administration. It is nothing short of a miracle that given these obstacles, outstanding athletes like Obadele Thompson and Andrea Blackett emerged on the world stage. Others wait in the wings.

Fitness is also an integral part of the everyday life of many Bajans. There are a number of health gyms and fitness clubs open to both locals and visitors all year round.

o get uncorked

Those who live for the evening will not be disappointed with Barbados, as this is one Caribbean island where the clock does not stop. Variety is the spice of Bajan nightlife! From a romantic drink beneath a moonlit sky to the frenetic tropical beat of the nightclub scene, there is plenty of entertainment for everyone. It is said there are over a thousand drinking houses in Barbados – there may even be more – nobody is counting! There are certainly hundreds of rum shops scattered throughout the island, many within a stone's throw of each other. They date back to the origins of this golden liquid – the nectar of the mighty sugar cane – which moulded the island's economic history.

Favourite libations

The world-famous Mount Gay rum was in production over 300 years ago, and 'rum shops' evolved as essential resting spots for hard-working, hard-drinking men. Over time, the rum shops expanded their merchandise to become almost community shops, and some entrepreneurial owners have even attempted to embrace the tourism industry. However, most rum shops remain essentially parochial, community-based, and the continuing domain of hard-drinking Bajan men. Rum is a great buy in Barbados and visits to Mount Gay (*see Sightseeing Spectacular, page 51*); Malibu, Cockspur, and the impressive Four Square Rum factory complex offer excellent opportunities to visit the factory floor, learn a little of the history, and, of course, indulge!

And *how* to indulge? Most visitors enjoy rum punch, while the hardened locals prefer rum and water. Socialites, on the other hand, opt for rum and coke.

But if your favourite tipple is beer, then get acclimatised to Banks beer as soon as you arrive. The national beer of Barbados has few competitors – although Carib, Red Stripe, and Piton beers provide Caribbean alternatives. Draught Banks beer is available, but few bars serve it in pint glasses. The **Red Rooster** bar, a lively English-style pub on the south coast, is an exception.

Pick up your free Banks Beer Trail Brochure and then follow the trail to earn a complimentary tour of the brewery, a Banks hat, or a Banks T-shirt.

Barbados has a wide range bars and restaurants. Drinks are essentially the same everywhere, but prices vary according to the establishment. The same Banks Beer that costs around a dollar in a St. Lucy rum shop may cost six times as much at an exclusive west coast hotel.

Fun cruises on the ***Jolly Roger*** pirate ship, or catamaran cruises like ***Heatwave***, offer unlimited drinks and an excellent buffet

Below: Chester, the award-winning barman at the Mount Gay factory demonstrates the art of tasting vintage rum.

lunch. The **Harbour Lights** nightclub has all-inclusive evenings where guests pay an entrance fee at the door and drink free until 3am.

Of a more cultural nature, the *Tropical Spectacular* and *1627 and All That* shows combine dinner and drinks with a superb evening's entertainment featuring spectacular costumes, music and dance, limbo-dancing, stilt-walkers, and fire-eating.

So why not uncork yourself the whole way round Barbados? Start in downtown Bridgetown, the commercial hub of Barbados, where the Careenage brings the Caribbean Sea right into the city centre. Independence Arch overlooks the multitude of anchored charterboats, fishing boats, and catamarans – and from it you can almost fall into the **Rusty Pelican**, a lively first-floor restaurant and bar that has an unrivalled view of bustling Bridgetown. Prop up the bar or opt for an outside table and enjoy the live music, which is performed most nights.

Just below the Rusty Pelican, the cobblestone quayside leads to the **Waterfront Café** – a Parisian-style restaurant, with a great reputation for food, music, and atmosphere. Frequent art exhibitions (a passion of the owner Sue Walcott) and lively jazz sessions add to the appeal of this bustling establishment.

Out of the city

Barbados has a few downtown bars, but there is much more fun to be had outside the city centre.

Heading north towards the west coast up Spring Garden Highway, leads to Brighton Beach and **Weiser's Beach Bar** – the hub of

watersports activities during the day. The bar buzzes in the evening with drinkers and diners. Happy hour on Fridays from 4–7pm is a must.

A mile further north, the roundabout offers an inland option to Bridgetown suburbia, but stay on track for the 'platinum strip' and head up the coast road. Look for the **Thirsty Duck**, nestling beneath shady coconut trees opposite the Esso garage. This hideaway bar is owned and run by the delightful Gloria and Roger, whose parting cocktails are not to be missed.

Moving further north, the west coast is alive with watersports and sunseekers in the daytime and humming with activity during the evening. **Bourbon Street** sits on the beach and is the island's top restaurant for Cajun cooking, as well as being a great place to listen to jazz. The **Bamboo Beach Bar** is another haunt along this part of the coast. It is an old favourite with seasoned visitors, but it has lost some of its charm since it was absorbed into the Tamarind Hotel complex.

A few hundred yards beyond, a green-and-yellow chattel house is home to **Crocodile's Den**. This vibrant sports bar is owned by former jockey Harry Hinds. They also serve great food late into the night. Like nearby Bomba's Beach Bar, it is a favourite haunt of the rich and famous.

The nearby **Coachouse** has been a thriving bar for years. Live entertainment attracts locals to enjoy a great pub atmosphere, as well as good food. Head to the **Casbah** nightclub at Baku Beach in Sunset Crest, five minutes up the road. If disco dancing, drinking, and socialising tops your priority list, then this Turkish-style nightclub will fit the bill.

The fashionable St. James houses many of the 'in places', as well as some of the most exclusive hotels on the island. For elegance, sophistication, and exclusivity, the cocktail bars of the **Coral Reef**, **Royal Pavillion**, and **Glitter Bay** may be your idea of heaven on earth – and why not if a more peaceful atmosphere beckons.

The nearby **Lone Star Restaurant** also welcomes smartly-dressed non-diners in either their elegant beach bar or the air-conditioned Bellini and Cocktail Bar. They offer a superlative selection of fine champagne, as well as many great wines. This is a fabulous spot to watch to sunset sipping tasty tropical cocktails.

Holetown haunts

For variety and choice, there is no better place to head for than 1st and 2nd streets in Holetown. The bar in **Olives Restaurant** is a spacious, relaxing area full of tropical plants and furnished with comfortable rattan chairs.

Raggamuffins is a compact chattel house bar and restaurant where the delightful owners, Neil and Nuru serve a range of exciting cocktails. Paul and Annie Matthews own the colourfully-painted **Angry Annie's**. This charming couple from Birmingham, England are delightful hosts who provide excellent service and great food.

Mullins Beach Bar, further up the coast in St. Peter, is a favourite in these parts. Many a visit to this stunning location has developed into lunch or dinner, and numerous repeat visits. Combined with a beautiful beach and friendly locals, there can be few nicer places to watch the sunset. The drinks are

reasonably priced and it is definintely a place one will find hard to leave.

Further north in the old town of Speightstown is the **Fisherman's Pub**. This open-air seaside establishment is a great place to relax with a cold beer and enjoy some excellent sensibly-priced Bajan cooking. The atmosphere is relaxed and the dress casual.

The bar at the **Cobbler's Cove** hotel serves a fantastic array of colourful and exotic cocktails, (*see photograph below*). This serene setting on the west coast is a tranquil oasis away from the bustle of St.Lawrence Gap.

The east coast

The night-life on the Barbados entertainment map effectively ends at Speightstown. While the adventurous traveller might venture across to the east coast, it is unlikely to be for a night out. However, sightseeing is thirsty work and the numerous rum shops scattered island-wide provide welcome refreshment for weary travellers. Most are poorly signposted, although for enterprise and initiative, one St. Andrew's lady deserves special mention. Aptly-named **Nigel Benn's Auntie's Pub**, this establishment takes a little finding but once located at the foot of Farley Hill, the journey is worth it – local culture at its best!

Night-life on the east coast contrasts as sharply with the west coast as its surf. Even on such a small island, Bajans do not like to travel far. Yet the choppy waters of Bathsheba and the 'Soup Bowl' provide the **Edgewater Hotel** and **Round House Restaurant** with unrivalled panoramic views.

These spots are ideal for a quick drink, but if you want to get closer to the magnificent coastline, then join the locals and surfers at the **Bonito Bar** in Bathsheba. The beer is cheap and the buffet lunches good value. **Struggles Bar** at East Point, not far from the lighthouse, rises like an oasis in rural south-east Barbados. It is easy to see why refreshment stops at Struggles are popular, although both **Sam Lord's Castle** and the **Crane Beach Hotel** are also worth a visit and provide breathtaking views.

Travelling back along the south coast, the night-life reappears in Oistins, where the Friday night open-air fish fry has captured the imagination of the informal entertainment industry. Akin to a huge impromtu street party, there is plenty of music, dance, and delicious fresh fish! Meet Ermine, who will tell you that the best way to cook flying fish is to put a little rum in the batter. Definitely no arguing with that!

For many visitors, the hub of Bajan night-life is St Lawrence Gap although in reality the entertainment 'strip' extends right up to Bridgetown.

The Gap is brimming with restaurants, bars, music, street vendors, traffic, and fast-food stalls. It also has three of the island's most popular night-spots virtually next-door to each other.

The **Ship Inn** is the favourite haunt of many visitors and boasts top music and live bands on most evenings. This bustling pub has grown over the last thirty years to encompass two spacious bars and an open-air courtyard. It is one of the best-known night-spots in Barbados and has an excellent reputation for good food – particularly the steaks, chicken and seafood.

McBride's is an authentic Irish pub that quickly fills up most evenings. It has a lively atmosphere and a small dance floor. They also serve good, reasonably-priced food.

After Dark is three clubs all in one. The best nights are when open-air live shows are performed in the huge courtyard. Barbados has a rich tradition for top-class popular Caribbean music and bands like Krosfyah, Square One, Coalition, For The People, and Biggy Irie and the Israelites pull crowds wherever they perform.

Before leaving this side of the Gap, if you want to watch the world go by and sip frozen margaritas, then **Café Sol** on the corner is the ideal venue. A order of nachos with cheese accompanied by a few Mexican specialities will complete your pleasure.

The top of the Gap is the hub of Bajan night-life, but further along the **Southern Palms** and **Casuarina** hotels provide family entertainment in a congenial and relaxing atmosphere.

The 'strip'

From St Lawrence Gap to Bridgetown there is no shortage of hotels, beach bars, sports bars, restaurants, and nightclubs. The **Carib Beach Bar** has one of the best locations on the popular Sandy Beach. It combines a relaxed, casual atmosphere with great food, particularly the fish. James, the proprietor (and national rugby fly half) makes visitors extremely welcome. A favourite with hardy locals, the Carib is a good place to meet people and enjoy Bajan hospitality. They have special nights and fun days, such as the Highland Games in May as part of the Celtic Festival.

The **Lucky Horseshoe**, with its multitude of television screens and slot machines, has a lively Wild West atmosphere. It serves

tasty ribs and great steaks. There is also a quieter lounge upstairs.

Bubba's is a high-tech sports bar with vast screens transmitting top sporting events from around the world. They also show Disney cartoons during the family breakfast on Sunday mornings. **Bert's Bar**, is more relaxed and offers everything for the sports enthusiast. Bert, himself, is a great connonisseur of ball games and is one of the most reliable sources of breaking news from around the island!

Champers, **Shak Shak**, and **39 Steps** are better known as top-class restaurants, but like most dining establishments in Barbados, they also welcome casual drinkers. The **Red Rooster**, opposite the Coconut Court Hotel, is modelled on a traditional English pub and serves the best beer in Barbados in convivial

surroundings. Happy Hour here has been known to stretch to the next day! Owner Mandy Blades, combines great food with a true pub atmosphere and warm hospitality, which is hardly surprising as she is the daughter of a pub owner in London.

The **Harbour Lights** is the top nightclub on the island, and has been that way for over twenty years. Mondays are 'beach party' nights, but the best value evenings are the all-inclusives.

The **Boatyard** sits alongside beautiful Carlisle Bay and thrives on live entertainment. It has a bustling bar and is the place for much late night revelry. Tip a barman early to ensure speedy service for the whole evening. The best place to sit is out in the courtyard, where it is much cooler when the place gets packed. Don't miss happy hour, and be sure to sample the excellent fish cakes.

The Boatyard is just several hundred yards from the Careenage and Independence Square – just the place to stumble into the Rusty Pelican and start all over again!

eat your

Barbados has an incredible variety of places to eat and the Bajan restaurant business is booming. The island enjoys the talents of many creative chefs who have successfully combined an eclectic mix of local seafood, vegetables, fruits and spices with European and Asian techniques to produce a sophisticated and modern Caribbean cuisine.

Fresh fish and seafood usually account for the majority of specials appearing on menus and snapper, lobster, tuna and mahi mahi are some of the local delights which are served in delicious, modish sauces. Chicken and meat dishes all figure, along with a good selection of pasta and vegetarian dishes.

heart out

It is also well-worth trying the local cuisine during your stay. Speciality dishes to sample include flying fish, dorado, hot salt fish cakes, pickled breadfruit, and pepperpot – the famous rich and spicy Caribbean stew. Barbadian food is usually highly seasoned and accompanied by rice, macaroni pie, plantain, cassava or yam. Also try the Caribbean speciality, the roti. This tasty dish which has its origins in India is a paper thin dough wrapped round a spicy mixture of either meat, chicken or fish (mind the bones which the locals like to chew on!).

The characteristics of the island's many restaurants varies greatly – ranging from luxurious venues in idyllic settings to more lively places in bustling surroundings.

There are many good restaurants and a recommended selection is given below. Each establishment has been rated for a three-course meal per head without drinks as either inexpensive (between B$40-50); moderate (between B$50-$60) and expensive (between B$60-90). Relax, enjoy the warmth of the welcoming atmosphere, the hospitality of the people and the delicious flavours of the island's vibrant and inspired food.

the island's finest

Try to book early as these restaurants are some of the most popular in Barbados.

The Lone Star Restaurant (Tel. 419-0599)

This prestigious restaurant is situated directly on the white sands of the west coast in St James and makes no pretence to be anything other than elegant, exclusive and chic. This is no ordinary restaurant and its fabulous location makes it undoubtedly one of the finest places to eat in the Caribbean. The imaginative owners have set an impressive standard which is reflected in the stylish decor, the splendid cooking, the charming staff and the superlative selection of champagnes and wines. The sophistication of the oceanfront *al fresco* dining deck provides an idyllic setting for either an informal lunch or a fairy tale evening to remember. The Bellini and cocktail bar, as well as the caviar and cigar bar add to a recipe for guaranteed success in this superb establishment.

The Lone Star's executive chef, Andy Whiffen is a culinary genius who turns every dish into a sensational work of art. Creative, gifted and highly professional in his approach, this master chef has devised a multicultural menu which is a blend of modern European, Mediterranean and Caribbean. A feeling of confidence underlies such harmonious dishes as seared tuna served rare with wasabi mash and vegetable spring rolls, or roast clams Louisiana style. Other intensely-flavoured specials include the slow-roasted duck, marinated in spiced red wine, served with a vegetable compote or Thai chicken and shrimp green curry served with perfectly-cooked fragrant rice. The Lone Star enjoys a fine reputation for their authentic Indian dishes that range from a creamy chicken tikka masala to outstanding aromatic fish and meat baltis – all served with traditional Indian breads, chutney and pilau rice. The delicious tandoori shrimp salad with mint yoghurt dressing is a perfect light alternative for seriously hot days! The less adventurous palette also has an wide choice in tasty Lone Star sandwiches. Selections include a hearty club sandwich with roast turkey, bacon, slow roasted

Opposite: Delicately-flavoured lobster and crab beignets drizzled with a sweet-and-sour sauce. Centre: The Lone Star Restaurant sits on a stretch of white sand beach on the west coast of Barbados.

tomatoes and mixed greens or classic burgers served with excellent thin crisp fries.

The Lone Star is a must for seafood devotees and the menu promises an impressive array of sparklingly-fresh oysters imported from the United States and Europe, dressed crab, freshwater crayfish, Maine lobster (in season), stone crab claws, Alaskan crab legs, as well as local shellfish delights. The hot seafood dishes are spectacular

Above: Delicious balti dishes are a favourite at the Lone Star Restaurant and are flavoured with an inspired blend of herbs and spices. Opposite: Raw salmon sashimi is served with zesty wasabi and soy sauce.

and include such vibrant flavour combinations as moules marinière with garlic bread, pan fried shrimps in a delicately spiced butter or herb-glazed mussels with mixed local leaves.

The caviar bar is the only one of its kind on the island and the exquisite beluga, oscietre or sevruga caviar is imported from Iran and served with blinis, new potatoes and sour cream.

Desserts concentrate on exemplary productions of simple classics and feature seductive options as white chocolate cheesecake with a zingy summerfruit sauce; chargrilled

peaches with vanilla sugar and mascarpone or ginger crème brûlée served with raspberries.

Staff convey the right balance of formality and easy-going friendliness and the excellent wine list offers good drinking at all price levels. It boasts a varied choice ranging from sunny New world whites to serious red Bordeaux and burgundies. Chile, Italy and Spain are given due consideration too. There is also an exceptional range of *grand marque* champagnes.

Fans of the Lone Star will be interested to note that west London is home to two other restaurants in the group. *The Wharf* in Teddington, Middlesex (Tel: 0181-977-6333), based on the Lone Star's nautical theme and the Mediterranean-style *Prego*, in Richmond, Surrey (Tel: 0181-948 8508) are both worth visiting on a trip to this side of the capital. (*Expensive*)

The Carambola Restaurant (Tel: 432-0832)

The Carambola sits on a stunning cliff-top setting in St. James and most of the tables offer an idyllic view of the Caribbean Sea. Subtle lighting concealed behind lush foliage adds a magical touch to this already splendid location where diners are always guaranteed an unforgettable evening. The cooking is essentially gourmet European with Caribbean flair, and the fish and seafood dishes are refined and technically excellent. The extensive menu combines a wonderful selection of locally-grown and imported produce, all served in a classical, but innovative style. (*Expensive*)

Olives (Tel: 432-2112)

Holetown has an excellent selection of restaurants and many visitors to Barbados have happily wined and dined on 1st and 2nd streets without venturing further afield during their entire stay. Olives is the showpiece of Larry and Michelle Rogers' restaurant empire, which also includes *La Terra* at Baku Beach and the nearby *Kitchen Korner*. This tastefully-decorated traditional Holetown townhouse provides both inside and courtyard dining. The upstairs bar, with its lofty ceilings, is a particular favourite with patrons and serves tasty bar snacks. Larry has an artistic flair for imaginative cooking and has created some superb dishes. Try the wafer-thin beef carpaccio, seared tuna or one of the piping

hot fresh pasta dishes. A cosmopolitan collection of wines spreads its favours between France and the New World. (*Moderate-Expensive*)

The Cliff (Tel: 432-1922)

The excellent reputation and world-acclaimed culinary talents of Paul Owens have made this establishment a favourite of the gliteratti. Exquisite food, combined with an enchanting waterfront setting and excellent service are the hallmarks of this magnificent restaurant. Set on a cliff-top at Derricks in St. James, on the exclusive west coast, the location sets the scene for a gastronomic journey. The creative and superbly-presented cuisine is wide ranging and thoroughly inspired. The classically based menu incorporates some contemporary touches, and lightness, refinement and precision are hallmarks of the cooking. The seafood dishes are

beautifully cooked in flavoursome sauces and retain all their fine flavour and texture. Richness and a degree of luxury are the norm, evident in the meat and game dishes. The Cliff has, without doubt, all the elements to turn any evening into a memorable occasion. (*Expensive*)

shrimps with a tangy, mango salsa. Pasta and meat also feature prominently and are prepared in an imaginative style with spices and herbs. Standards are consistently high. (*Expensive*)

The Bagatelle Restaurant (Tel: 421-6767)

For something completely different, the Bagatelle Restaurant gives diners a rare opportunity to sample the ambience and lifestyle of a bygone era. The Bagatelle Great House was built around 1645 and is now a protected asset of the Barbados National Trust. It is a classic example of Barbadian architecture and the cool restaurant overlooks verdant tropical gardens. Owners Richie and Val Richings have created a delightful restaurant which serves an inspired menu made up of a fusion of Caribbean and European flavours. (*Expensive*)

Champers (Tel: 435-6644)

Champers in Hastings is located right on the water's edge and is an oasis for fine food and wine. The fashionable bar on the ground floor is a great place to enjoy a bottle of wine and the

tasty fare listed on the daily-changing list of specials. The more formal dining room upstairs offers spectacular views of the south coast and serves a contemporary menu which is worthy of its good reputation. Cheryl and Sophie Ann are the charming hostesses, and their friendly bar staff are extremely adept at creating delicious tropical cocktails. (*Moderate*)

Shak-Shak (Tel: 435-1284)

This elegant oceanfront restaurant is a definite must for its fabulous location and exotic menu. Chef, Guy Beasley, has his finger on the pulse of modern cooking and serves an interesting mix of seafood and fish specialities, as well as freshly-made soups and salads. Try to book a table right on the water's edge. (*Moderate*)

Pisces Restaurant (Tel: 435-6564)

Pisces overlooks a picturesque little bay that shimmers against the lights of the surrounding buildings and traffic. It has an unrivalled reputation for excellent and sparkingly-fresh seafood, superbly prepared using home-grown herbs, spices and fruits. The quaint wooden building

La Maison (Tel: 432-1156)

La Maison in Holetown offers international gourmet cooking in a pretty beachfront setting. This award-winning restaurant housed in a beautiful coral stone building is a particular favourite of many visitors. The seafood dishes are first-rate and include superbly-cooked lobster in a zesty lime sauce or spiced

Above: Freshly-baked breads served with an olive tapenade and aïoli. Opposite: An appetizing tomato and chilli galette provides a tasty vegetarian alternative.

which extends along the bay is packed with lush tropical plants and a fabulous collection of paintings by local artists. Desserts range from the tried-and-true to some decadent specials. (*Expensive*)

simpler fare

Despite its reputation for sophisticated and expensive cuisine, there are many restaurants in Barbados that offer excellent, reasonably-priced simple food.

The leading fast-food chain in Barbados is **Chefette Restaurants** and branches are found in ten locations scattered around the island. The food is good value, and freshly prepared. They serve great broasted chicken, tasty burgers, sandwiches, rotis and excellent milk shakes. Some locations have 'drive-throughs' and four have enclosed adventure playgrounds for children. **Barbecue Barn** is part of the Chefette chain and serves barbecued steaks, chicken or fish with jacket potatoes, fries or rice. There is also an excellent salad bar offering a huge range of fresh vegetables and delicious salad dressings. They are in three locations: Rockley, Christ Church

(Tel: 430-3402); Holetown, St. James (Tel: 419-8652); Warrens, St. Michael (417-8552).

Ideal Restaurant (Tel: 431-2139)

A welcome break for shoppers is the Ideal Restaurant on the top floor of the Cave Shepherd Building in Broad Street, Bridgetown. They offer generous helpings of genuine Bajan food and the place is popular with both locals and visitors. Try the Bajan beef stew with peas and rice, macaroni pie, fried plantain, and a complimentary side salad. (*Inexpensive*)

Jeff Mex (Tel: 431 0857)

Jeff Mex is located in Broad Street and serves tasty Mexican specialities, as well as burgers, fresh sandwiches and salads. (*Inexpensive*)

The Roti Den (Tel: 435-9071)

Located at the entrance to St Lawrence Gap, the Roti Den is in a lovely setting. The roti is a chapati (stovetop-baked unleavened bread) wrapped around a curried meal of meat, fish, or chicken and potato. Vegetarian rotis are also served. (*Inexpensive*)

Bean 'n Bagel Café
(Tel: 420 4604)

This delightful café in St. Lawrence Gap is a perfect place to visit for a great breakfast or lunchtime snack. An excellent

range of flavoured coffees with delicious fresh sandwiches on speciality breads, fresh bagels and tasty pastries are the basis for the simple and reasonably-priced menu. Main meals include crab back salad, vegetarian quiche or a robust portion of lasagne. The café is decorated with hand-painted ceramic tiles and seating is either inside or outside on a sunny deck. (*Inexpensive*)

Fisherman's Pub (Tel:

The Fisherman's Pub in Speightstown has a long tradition for good Bajan food at a reasonable price. A seaside drinking spot is popular with both locals and visitors and the lunchtime servings of chicken, fish, or beef stew are delicious. (*Inexpensive*)

Pizzaz Pizza

Pizza is popular throughout Barbados and is always good value. Pizzaz Pizza has branches in Holetown (Tel. 432-0227) and Bridgetown (Tel. 428-6628). Pizzaz Pizza in Fontabelle is located in a colourful, airy building, and features a

Left: Chablis is an excellent wine to accompany the seafood specialities served around the island. Opposite: Red snapper in a tasty fresh basil and tomato sauce.

photograph gallery of some of the great moments in the history of West Indies cricket. (*Inexpensive*)

Oistins Fish Fry

In recent years the open-air fish fry has become the hallmark of this bustling south-coast fishing village. Rum shops, bars, and live entertainment set the scene as visitors drift from stall to stall to experience Bajan cooking at its best. Flying fish and chicken top the menu, but it is the relaxed, open-air ambience of the Oistins Fish Fry that makes it such a unique eating experience. (Inexpensive)

romantic restaurants

The Schooner (Tel: 426-4000)

Located in the scenic Carlisle Bay, a Victorian pier is an unusual, but charming setting for this restaurant whose specialities include imaginatively-prepared seafood specialities. There is a lobster aquarium, as well as an excellent selection of freshly-caught local fish. Each Saturday night there is a seafood gourmet dinner. For meat eaters, simplicity is their strength, yielding tender grilled steaks, as well as delicious lamb or duck delights. (*Expensive*)

Fathoms (Tel: 432-2568)

The tables sit beneath shady trees at this charming beachside restaurant in Paynes Bay. This is a perfect spot to watch the sunset, enjoy a few sundowners and stay on for a candlelit dinner. The impressive menu is predominately seafood and fish inspired, and diners will find the lobster- and crab-based dishes expertly cooked in fragrant herbs and spices. (*Expensive*)

Water's Edge (Tel: 428-7141)

The location of this delightful restaurant makes a striking impact on newcomers, and the food continues to impress. Scandanavian chef Nils Mannestedt serves an eclectic blend of imaginative dishes inspired by a fusion of flavours taken from around the globe. Specialities include chargrilled jumbo shrimp and pineapple kebabs served on jasmine rice with Thai red curry sauce, or smoked salmon interleaved with fresh shrimp, herbs, sour cream and caviar. Steaks are tender and perfectly cooked. (*Moderate-expensive*)

Sand Dollar (Tel: 435-6956)

This south coast establishment is situated on the popular Sandy Beach and offers a peaceful, romantic setting. The Gomes family have created a friendly atmosphere where modern Caribbean flavours are predominant. The menu favours the freshest of local seafood and fish as the basis for some simple, but alluring dishes. (*Moderate*).

Nico's (Tel: 432-6386)

A warm welcome awaits in this fabulous champagne and wine bar set amidst peaceful tropical gardens in St. James. The wine list features an excellent selection of champagnes, French and New World wines and diners can be sure of sampling some of the best food on the island. Seafood is a strong point and the extensive menu includes Nico's highly-acclaimed grilled lobster. (*Moderate-Expensive*)

Mango's by the Sea (Tel: 422-0704)

Mango's overlooks the Caribbean Sea at Speightstown and is an idyllic romantic hideaway. The menu is contemporary and fish figures prominently. The chef specialises in grilled lobster served in a variety of delicate sauces, or beautifully-tender

lively restaurants

Many people are looking for more than just gourmet cooking when they eat out, and a number of restaurants in Barbados are renowned for their lively service and first-class entertainment.

The Waterfront Café (Tel: 427-0093)

Situated on the waterside in Bridgetown, this friendly restaurant has a great reputation for fine food and excellent live music particularly jazz. The Dixie Land Jazz Band is a particular favourites, but all the most popular jazz musicians in Barbados feature sometime during the week, and the music continues until at least 2am. Owner, Sue Walcott has created a menu which features a number of savoury Bajan specialities and zesty creole dishes to provide an authentic flavour of the Caribbean. Try the classic pepperpot, a hot and spicy stew seasoned with cassareep, or the piquant fish pie, a delicious mix of flying fish and kingfish in a curry sauce topped with sweet potato and cheese. For a lighter snack, the tapas are highly recommended, as are the crab rissoles or ceviche – kingfish marinated in a zesty mix of lime and cucumber and served with melba toast. (*Moderate*)

The Rusty Pelican (Tel: 436 7778)

The Rusty Pelican, with its elevated view of Bridgetown is a fun spot and definitely NOT the place for a quiet, romantic evening. The style is all-embracing and some vibrant, punchy flavours are the result. Delicious offerings include pepper shrimp, drunken honey wings, succulent baby back ribs, tandoori chicken or freshly-grilled local fish. Lively music features on most evenings and reservations are essential for Friday nights. (*Moderate*).

Ragamuffins (Tel: 432-1295)

Located in a tiny authentic chattel house in Holetown, Ragamuffins's oozes with character and atmosphere. The charming owners, Neil and Nuru Patterson are on hand most nights to ensure the drinks, food and ambience are second to none but beware of Neil's lethal

steaks prepared in rich sauces and served with local vegetables. Gail and Pierre Spenard are extremely welcoming and the staff friendly. A complimentary shuttle service is available from all hotels and villas between Holetown and Mango's. (*Expensive*)

pre-dinner rum punch! The excellent menu, which roams the world for cross-cultural combinations that work incredibly well, has a strong Caribbean influence. Dishes include blackened shrimp, West Indian chicken curry and a delicious vegetarian stew. The shellfish and beautifully tender T-bone steaks are flawlessly cooked, and the ever-changing daily specials make return visits an absolute must. (*Moderate*)

Angry Annies (Tel: 432 2119)

Annie and Paul Matthews have created an exciting menu where traditional Bajan style has been successfully embraced and combined with Asian and oriental flavours. Try the heavily-spiced blackened fresh fish, or the more subtle tastes of lobster in mornay sauce, or rack of lamb simmered in mint and Dijon mustard. Annie's also has an excellent reputation for authentic curries served with an array of Indian appetizers. The pasta dishes are wonderful – particularly the spicy speciality known as Rasta Pasta. Delightful service compliments cheerful surroundings where it is easy to linger long into the evening enjoying chilled drinks and zesty food. (*Moderate*)

hotel restaurants

Most of the premier hotels in Barbados incorporate at least one first-rate restaurant, where highly-trained chefs serve sophisticated international cuisine in elegant and tasteful surroundings. The style is consistent and reliable and often features interesting variations that embrace the local flavours and produce. This guide has chosen (with a couple of exceptions) to feature independent restaurants which offer gastronomic experiences away from hotel dining. However, for those who prefer classical cooking accompanied by professional service in a memorable setting, the following hotel restaurants are worthy of note.

The Sandpiper (Tel. 422-2251)

Treasure Beach (Tel. 432-1346)

Coral Reef Club (Tel. 422-2372)

The Orchid Room at the Colony Club (Tel. 422-2335)

The Palm Terrace at the Royal Pavillion Hotel (Tel. 422-4444).

Piperade at the Glitter Bay Hotel (Tel. 422-4111)

Neptunes at Tamarind Cove (Tel. 432-1332)

Southern Palms (Tel. 428-7171)

Opposite: Prawns sautéed in a batter flavoured with ginger and spring onion on a bed of fresh local leaves. Below: Some of the finest Caribbean fruits of the sea.

global flavours

Tam's Wok (432-8000)

Located on 1st Street in Holetown, this lively establishment has carved out an excellent reputation for genuine Cantonese and Szechuan cooking. The menu provides tasty versions of seafood in ginger and garlic, fresh shrimp in chilli and excellent roast duck and chicken. Service is swift and friendly. *(Moderate)*.

Above and right: Full-bodied olive oil often appears on dining tables as a condiment to add to soups, salads, bread and vegetables.

Bourbon Street (Tel: 424-4557).

Bourbon Street in St. James brings the cooking of New Orleans to Barbados and atmosphere figures prominently in the appeal of this oceanfront setting. The Cajun cooking is authentic and inspire a fresh, tastebud-sharpening glow. Diners are treated to hearty jambalayas flavoured with fresh chilli and packed with the freshest of shellfish; oysters served with a piquant horseradish dressing, or Cajun blackened chicken. Robust and flavoursome cooking accompanied by the strains of blues and jazz make this cocktail bar and restaurant an excellent choice. *(Moderate-Expensive)*

Bellini's (Tel: 435-7246)

This attractive Italian restaurant overlooks the waters of St. Lawrence Gap and the menu offers some refined up-to-date Italian cooking. A range of fresh pastas are served, as well as excellent pizza and salads. The daily specials deal enthusiastically

in fresh seafood and meat options, and successfully avoids Italian clichés in favour of inspired appetizing flavours. *(Moderate-Expensive)*

Brown Sugar (Tel: 426-7684)

Located on Aquatic Gap, Brown Sugar offers one of the best Caribbean buffet lunches in Barbados which includes spicy beef pepperpot or robust fish stews. Set within a tropical atmosphere, this restaurant serves some of the tastiest seafood in the area. *(Expensive)*.

île de France (Tel: 422-3245)

This award-winning restaurant of international acclaim is set on the

oceanfront at the Settler's Beach Hotel in Holetown. Chef Michel has created an enterprising menu which deals largely in classical French regional cooking. Everything is produced with great assurance and dishes have been designed to reassure and comfort. Try the roast lobster flavoured with local spices and herbs, the wafer-thin fish carpaccio or the succulent rack of lamb. (*Expensive*).

Emerald Palm (Tel: 422-4116)

Chef, Tim Early has kept abreast of the times in creating a contemporary menu that juxtaposes culinary cultures and flavours from around the world. Set amidst lush tropical gardens at Porters, this is a delightful place to sample some outstanding cooking. An inventory of modish ingredients includes coriander butter, fresh chilli oil, yellow pepper aioli or orange and lime dressing, all of which which appear in carefully composed dishes such as Thai fish cakes, chargrilled scallops and baby squid, or seared tuna. (*Expensive*)

All dishes were styled and prepared by Andy Whiffen, the executive chef at the Lone Star Restaurant, near to Holetown.

SOME BAJAN SPECIALITIES

Life in Barbados has been shaped by many international influences and this is very much in evidence in the cooking. It is particularly creative because of the lack of native foods that are available and also because budgets are somewhat limited. The cooking has evolved into a hybrid of cooking traditions that look to England and Africa, as well as European, Asian and American techniques for its roots.

The Bajan national dish of *cou-cou* and salt fish originates from Africa. *Cou-cou* is a pudding made of cornmeal and water, flavoured with okra. Once mixed, it is turned out onto a plate, ladled with gravy and served with salted cod.

Flying fish

One of the island's staple foods, flying fish is readily available throughout most of the year. A spicy Bajan seasoning enhances the taste, whether fried, steamed, or baked. The seasoning is prepared from chopped onion, parsley, thyme, garlic, black and red pepper, paprika and lime juice. The fish are usually 7 to 9 inches (18 to 23 cm) long and are easily filleted. They can be served as a main course meal or in a tasty 'cutter' (bread roll).

Fish cakes

Made from dried and salted codfish, the fish cakes are prepared by mixing boiled and finely-minced cod with boiled pumpkin, grated raw yam, beaten eggs, milk, butter, salt, and pepper. The mixture is then fried in small balls to produce the tasty fish cakes sold throughout the island.

Peas and Rice

This is a popular staple dish. Rice is boiled with a variety of peas including green, blackeye, split peas or lentils. It is seasoned with salted meats and local spices.

Pudding and souse

This dish has been made for centuries and is found throughout the island. The pudding is made from sweet potato which is stuffed into a pig's intestines. It is then steamed and ends up resembling a long, dark sausage. This is cut into slices and served with the souse – the pig's head, feet and flesh which is cooked until tender and then pickled (soused) with lime juice, onion, salt, hot peppers and parsley.

Visitors to the Caribbean generally agree that Barbados is one of the most beautiful islands in the West Indies. The name alone conjures up glamour and a selection of the finest hotels and spectacular private villas await visitors to this magical island.

For detailed information on the hotels contact the **Barbados Hotel and Tourism Organisation** (Tel: 246-426-5041) or the **Barbados Tourism Authority** (Tel: 246-427-2623). There are also a number of guest houses and small hotel apartment blocks and the Barbados Tourism Authority can provide full details of the properties available.

The west coast is more renowned for attracting the glitterati, and is certainly where the more exclusive hotels and villas are located. A fabulous selection of accommodation is to be found on this exquisite 10 mile (16km) stretch of dazzling white-sand beach. There are many excellent restaurants and lively bars in this area.

Left: The fabulous crenelated towers of the Cobbler's Cove Hotel which was built early in the nineteenth century by a Bajan sugar baron. Right: The Camelot suite is lavishly decorated and offers fabulous sea views from a private sundeck.

hang your hat

Cobbler's Cove Hotel

Tel: 422 2291. Fax 422 1460
e-mail: cobblers@caribsurf.com

The stunning Cobbler's Cove Hotel sits majestically on the north-west shores of Barbados amidst verdant secluded gardens of golden palm, travellers' and banana trees.

This tropical haven is run by the charming long-serving manager Hamish Watson who maintains continual high standards in this serene environment away from the bustle of the south coast. All the suites are spacious and comfortable with sitting rooms that open fully to a terrace through sliding doors. Each has a small dining area, a concealed kitchenette with full wet bar, and living room, as well as a separate air-conditioned bedroom and bathroom. The bedrooms are simply, but elegantly furnished, with homely touches.

The Camelot suite with its crenelated towers bears a distant resemblance to a European castle and is opulently furnished. It has its own pool, sea views and a four-poster king size bed. The adjoining Colleton Suite is as equally lavish and handsomely-decorated in relaxing tones of blue and cream.

The hotel has a reputation for fine cooking and dishes range from a medley of local seafood sautéed in butter and garlic to mouth-watering steaks in green pepper sauce. The tables are set in an airy pavillion overlooking the sea and the freshwater pool. Each evening an à la carte menu is available, as well as a table d'hôte five course dinner. The hotel staff are extremely helpful and go out of their way to ensure that guests needs are met with courtesy and warmth.

The usually-deserted beach sits just beyond the grounds where snorkelling, windsurfing, sunfish sailing and water-skiing are available.

Further down the 'platinum' coast, the Royal Pavilion and Glitter Bay are two other hotels from the top drawer of Bajan hospitality. Originally built and owned by energetic entrepreneur Michael Pemberton, both properties are now owned by the large Canadian group, Princess Hotels.

The Glitter Bay Hotel

Tel: 422-4111. Fax: 422 3940

The Glitter Bay is the smaller and more intimate of the two using a Great House, originally owned by Sir Edward Cunard the shipping magnate, as its reception area. The grounds are spectacular and modelled on Italianate palazzo gardens. The hotel provides all the facilities one would expect from a

luxury establishment. The rooms all have outdoor patios or balconies that overlook the gardens, and larger suites are also available. There is also a delightful five-bedroom coral stone villa that sits on the edge of the beach where guests may either rent a room or take over the entire place!

The *Piperade* restaurant is a charming place to sample Caribbean cuisine blended with subtle Californian flavours.

The Royal Pavilion
Tel: 422 4444. Fax: 422 0118

The pink-and-white Royal Pavilion is a magnificent property that sits on the water's edge. Guests enter the complex along an impressive drive lined with stately royal palms. With its high, pitched ceilings, Palladian windows and lush greenery, the reception area exudes an air of opulence and grace. The rooms are equally glamorous and offer some of the finest ocean views in Barbados.

Above: The magnificient Royal Pavillion is a beautiful property that sits on the islanc's west coast. Opposite: The idyllic Lone Star Hotel enjoys a pristine picture-book setting on a peaceful stretch of sandy beach.

The decor is a tasteful blend of Mediterranean with West Indian accents and include all the facilities one could expect from a hotel in this league.

The open-air *Palm Terrace Restaurant* overlooks the ocean and re-creates the ambience of a bygone era. Guests dine on traditional French cuisine that has been fused with Caribbean flavours and ingredients. The delicious pan-fried lobster medallions with lime and pawpaw salsa are worthy of mention.

The watersports facilities at both the Glitter Bay and the Royal Pavillion are superb and include snorkelling, water-skiing, windsurfing, as well as scuba diving and small-craft sailing.

The Coral Reef Club
Tel: 422 2372.
Fax: 422 1776

The Coral Reef Club is a secluded family-run hotel set in in twelve acres of luxuriant gardens, shaded by by mahogany, flamboyant and casuarina trees. This oasis of calm purveys an atmosphere of total relaxation where guests can enjoy the ultimate in privacy during their stay. During 1999 the hotel underwent a US$10 million re-development programme which included the construction of a sparkling new pool and seventeen rooms – four of which of luxury "plantation suites". These suites are some of the finest resort accommodation in the region with an elegant living area that leads onto a covered terrace. The bedrooms feature either a canopied or four-poster bed, walk-in closet, luxurious bathroom, satellite television, video, fax machine, hi-fi system and a complimentary starter bar. The architectural style features shuttered windows, fretwork and French doors. There are also cottage-style rooms or suites decorated in the bright colours synonymous with the Caribbean.

The restaurant and lounge in the main house purvey the atmosphere of an elegant English club and the piano bar is a charming place to relax and sip tropical cocktails. The menu is varied and ranges from Bajan specialiaties, to traditional roast beef with Yorkshire pudding!

Some watersports are complimentary from the hotel's own stretch of beach, although a charge is made for water-skiing and Scuba diving.

The Sandpiper

Tel: 422 2251. Fax: 422 0900

The Sandpiper is an associate hotel of the Coral Reef Club and is one of the most exclusive small hotels in the West Indies. It provides a perfect holiday hideaway on the island's west coast. The one- and two-bedroom suites are all spacious and handsomely furnished.

The hotel shares a beach with the Coral Reef Club which stretches for miles in both directions. The hotel has a well justified reputation for meticulous service and a delightful staff who treat every guest with personal warmth and care.

The Lone Star Hotel

Tel: 419 0599
Fax: 419 0597
e-mail: lonestargarage@caribsurf.com

This stylish hotel is located directly on the beach in St. James, just north of Holetown.

No expense has been spared in the creation of an environment where guests are cossetted in a haven of rarified tranquillity. The hotel comprises just four luxuriously-appointed oceanfront suites that are a fine example of architectural innovation that is both practical and imaginative. Each suite features a king-size bed and a Philip Stark designed bathroom that includes a

six foot square shower. Suites are also uniquely equipped with a private fax machine for visitors wishing to keep in contact with the outside world, as well as a separate direct telephone line for modem hook-up. They also have a television, video player, hi-fi system, hair-dryer and safe.

The air-conditioned minimalist suites are chic, modern and comfortable and incorporate indigo and white furnishings that contrast starkly with dark purple heart wooden floors. The soothing and restrained decor tastefully augments this already perfect hideaway. Fridges, stocked with complimentary mineral water, beer and soft

This tiny hotel is for the romantic, the artist, the sunseeker or anyone looking to escape from reality. On an island which features a number of small resorts, the Lone Star is the undoubted jewel in the crown.

drinks, are restocked daily. There are also facilities for making hot drinks. The expansive terraces offer spectacular views and provide a blissful setting to watch the sun set.

A few steps lead to the beach and the magnificent Lone Star Restaurant. *(See Eat your Heart Out, page 127)*. Breakfast is served either in your suite or on the *al fresco* dining deck.

While the accent is definitely on getting away from it all, there are plenty of watersports activities for more energetic guests. Complimentary snorkelling, waterskiing and windsurfing is available and Scuba diving excursions to the island's pristine reefs, horse-back riding and golf can be arranged through the hotel's charming staff.

The Casuarina
Tel: 428-3600. Fax: 428 1970

The Casuarina is set within vibrant tropical gardens – the pride and joy of horticulturalist owner Bonnie Cole. This friendly 160-room apartment hotel is popular with families. A stroll through the shady gardens leads to a vast white-sand beach where a variety of watersports await. There is a varied range of accommodation ranging from beach front studios to one- or two-bedroom garden view apartments. The hotel offers a superb entertainment and comprehensive activities programme which includes 5am bicycle treks along the east coast with Bonnie! The restaurants serves authentic Bajan food, and there is a delightful piano bar

where guests can enjoy afternoon tea or early evening cocktails. Take note of the many original paintings hanging in the public areas of the hotel – Bonnie is an avid collector.

Bougainvillea Beach Resort
Tel: 418-0990. Fax: 418 0995

The Bougainvillea Beach Resort sits on a golden sandy beach shaded by casuarina trees. The hotel features tropical gardens with plunging waterfalls, as well as linked swimming pools with a sunken bar. The brightly furnished air-conditioned rooms, and the hotel's reputation for quality service make this hotel an ideal choice for families.

The Treasure Beach
Tel: 432-1346. Fax: 432 1094

The Treasure Beach is a peaceful privately-owned hotel set amidst immaculate gardens that lead to a fine stretch of sandy beach on the west coast. This charming twenty-nine room hotel is a sophisticated and discreet oasis away from the exuberance of the west coast revellry. The guest rooms form a horseshoe shape around the sparkling freshwater swimming pool. The rooms are a blend of fresh tropical coloursand all have air conditioning and ceiling fan. The hotel has a fine reputation for its excellent restaurant which overlook the gardens. The award-winning chef has introduced flavours from a variety of international cuisines and combines these with traditional Bajan dishes.

The Crane Beach Hotel
Tel: 423-6220. Fax: 432 5343
e-mail: cranebeach@sunbeach.net

The Crane Beach Hotel has attracted visitors since 1887 and, with its spectacular cliff-top setting and magnificent beach, it remains one of the most dramatic settings in the Caribbean. This romantic family-run hotel is on the windswept east coast and was the first resort hotel in Barbados. It is renowned for its old-world charm and the raw beauty of its surroundings. There are eighteen coral stone suites furnished with antiques and many rooms have four-poster beds.

Villa Nova
Tel: 433-1524

This romantic option is billed as the Caribbean's foremost five-star country resort hotel. This former colonial villa, built in 1834, was once owned by former British Prime Minister Sir Anthony

Eden, and its impressive list of former guests includes Queen Elizabeth, Sir Winston Churchill, and Noel Coward. Set in the tropical woodland of central Barbados, Villa Nova's peaceful seclusion has been tastefully moulded into an exclusive hotel. In 1998, it underwent a US$10 million refurbishment and seventeen junior suites and eleven one-bedroom suites have been added along with conference facilities, a library and fitness room. There are three restaurants in the resort.

The **Hilton Hotel** (Tel: 426-0200) at Needham's Point, overlooking Carlisle Bay, is still the business people's favourite hotel and also a popular resort for American visitors. Conveniently located overlooking Bridgetown, its cannons symbolically guard the commercial hub of Barbados. A major renovation programme started in the spring of 1999.

Opposite; Each stylish bedroom at the Lone Star Hotel leads onto a spacious terrace that sits directly above the beach. Below: The Crane Beach Hotel overlooks a wide stretch of sand on the island's rugged Atlantic coastline.

All Inclusives

Some people love them, but others remain dubious at the idea of spending their entire vacation within the confines of a single resort. The choice is obviously personal – although all-inclusive resorts have moved a long way from the days of accommodating only couples or those who crave over-indulgence of every kind to fulfil their holiday requirements!

Barbados offers a variety of all-inclusive resorts, some of which have arrangements that allow their guests to dine at other locations around the island. This has proved popular, because no resort could realistically hope to capture the true essence of the island within one compound.

Above: Sam Lord's Castle is a rambling resort on the south-east coast.

Almond Beach Village (Tel: 422-4900) at Speightstown is the best known all-inclusive resort on the island and offers a comprehensive package of activities covering watersports, golf, tennis, dining, and live entertainment.

The **Almond Beach Club** (Tel: 432-7840) is an associated resort located in fashionable St James. Set in 4 acres (1.5 hectares) of tropical gardens, it has two restaurants and four bars.

Sam Lord's Castle Resort

(Tel: 423-7350) is a majestic rambling complex on the south-east coast 6 miles (10 km) from Grantley Adams Airport. Legendary tales abound of Sam Lord, the 18th-century landowner who amassed great fortune by plundering ships off Long Bay. His former residence is a grand plantation house which is now the focal point of the 72-acre resort and the colonial setting for fine banquets, at which stories of the infamous pirate are related.

The rooms are modern and decorated in tasteful pastel colours. Most have ocean views and balconies. Rooms furnished with four-poster beds and antiques are available in the Castle itself at an additional charge to guests.

Queen Elizabeth and Prince Philip dined there during a visit, and an authentic re-creation of their seven-course repast is one of the many specials available. The Pirates' Shipwreck Party and the Bajan Fiesta are also two particular favourites with visitors.

For golfers and sports lovers, **Club Rockley** (Tel: 435-7880) is an ideal location with a nine-hole golf course. The well-furnished condominiums all have their own pool and bar facilities.

Other all-inclusive resorts include the **Mango Bay Hotel and Beach Club** at Holetown (Tel: 432-1384); the **Escape Hotel** (Tel: 424-7571) at Prospect; the **Island Inn** (Tel: 436-6393) close to Carlisle Bay; the **Welcome Inn Beach Hotel** (Tel: 424-9900) in Maxwell

Coast Road; and the Elegant Hotels group of the **Crystal Cove Hotel** (Tel: 432-2683), **Coconut Creek Hotel** (Tel: 432-0803) **Colony Club** (Tel: 422-2335) and **Turtle Beach Resort** (Tel: 428-7131). The Crystal Cove, Colony Club and Coconut Creek are on the west coast, while the Turtle Beach is next to the Casuarina on the south coast. The four hotels provide a total of 560 rooms and pride themselves on their efficient and helpful service, wide and varied selection of dining options and extensive facilities.

Apartment Hotels

There are a number of apartment hotels on the island and those worth mentioning include the **Rostrevor Apartments** (Tel: 428-9298) in St. Lawrence Gap, **St. Lawrence Apartments** (East and West, Tel: 435-6950), and the **Dover Beach Apartment Hotel** (Tel: 428-8076).

Just along the coast road towards Bridgetown, there is a wide variety of accommodation. Some of the best value-for-money are the **Worthing Court Apartment Hotel** (Tel: 435-7910), the **Caribbee Beach Hotel** (Tel: 436-6232), **Crystal Waters** (Tel: 435-7514), and the **Abbeyville Hotel** (Tel: 435-7294).

Villas

Discriminating guests seeking ultimate privacy and total relaxation should consider renting one of the many villas on the island. Accommodation ranges from a two-bedroom cosy beach property to an eight-bedroom Sandy Lane mansion – complete with basketball court, squash court, tennis court, swimming pool, gym, snooker table, and lush tropical gardens. Barbados offers more luxury villas than any other Caribbean island. Contact one of the island's leading real estate companies, who will provide you with details of the available properties. The largest companies are **Alleyne, Aguilar & Altman** (Tel: 432-0840); **Realtors** (Tel: 432-6930); **Bajan Services** (Tel: 422-2618); and **J M Bladon, Ernst & Young** (Tel: 430-3790).

Properties range in size and location from beach-front villas to retreats set in tropical landscapes further inland.

Two prestigious developments offer an alternative rental option. The internationally acclaimed **Royal Westmoreland** complex (Tel: 422-5959), with its championship Robert Trent-Jones designed golf course, a few miles inland from the prestigious west coast, has some of the most luxurious properties in Barbados. With panoramic views of the north and west coastlines, the Royal Westmoreland is an exclusive retreat esconced in superbly-landscaped grounds.

Port St Charles houses an imaginative waterfront development that boasts a wide variety of watersports and provides the opportunity for sailing enthusiasts to moor their vessel on their own doorstep! This prestigious waterfront villa complex offers many features including elegant restaurants and shops, while its berthing facilities will eventually establish it as the third port of entry into Barbados. For further information contact Port St Charles (Tel: 419-1000).

Sugar Hill, a David Lloyd Resort Community, is a new luxury development offering over forty townhouse villas for rent around a central tennis, pool, and health club facility. The nearby **Sugar Hill Estate** is a more exclusive development which has large detached properties – some of which are available for rent.

Whatever your pleasure, this enchanting island in the Caribbean has the perfect place to suit your needs.

the nitty gritty

planning your trip

how to get there; fare information; tour operators; when to go; what to pack; vaccination and immunisation; visa/immigration requirements; airline essentials & comfort

on arrival

airports; airport taxes

getting around

by air; by bus; by bus; by car

getting acclimatized

climate; business hours; courtesy & respect; electricity; media; money; post & couriers; religion; telephone; time; tipping; what to buy; what to wear

staying alive

health requirements; travel assistance and insurance; beat the heat; tropical diseases and cautions; personal security & safety; emergencies; hospitals; dentists; embassies and consultates

tourist information

Barbados tourist board
Barbados tourist offices overseas

Unlike its volcanic neighbours, Barbados is an unquestionably beautiful coral island basking in the warm turquoise waters of the Caribbean Sea.

An enchanting mix of rolling cane fields, colourful villages, spectacular beaches, welcoming people and a well-developed infrastructure make this one of the most popular holiday destinations in the West Indies. Its British heritage is still very much in evidence in Barbados where cricket and tea blend happily with calypso and rum. Tourism is a mainstay of the island's economy employing over ten thousand people. The islanders are a delightful and welcoming people and always happy to give advice or simply stop for a friendly chat!

Visitors intent on a memorable holiday have a fascinating range of choices to make. While dedicated cricket fans head for the Kensington Oval during a Test Match, serious and experienced surfers can brave the thundering Atlantic rollers on the east coast.

Sunseekers and watersports enthusiasts have seventy miles of coastline with innumerable beaches to explore. It is still possible to find a deserted place and relax and peace and solitude. After all the daytime activities, there is a wide choice of bars and restaurants in which to find refreshment, entertainment and excitement.

planning your trip

How to Get There

British Airways, Virgin Atlantic and BWIA are the only airlines to offer direct scheduled services from the UK; Condor offer a weekly direct flight from Frankfurt; LTU fly out of Dusseldorf and Martinair flies from Amsterdam. For a really memorable trip, remember that Barbados is one of the few destinations for British Airways Concorde flights

Charter flights are also available and are often are good value for direct flights to and from Barbados. Charter operators from the UK include Caledonian, Britannia and Monarch. Cheaper fares can also be obtained by flying through the US and changing planes – usually in Miami. Delta and American Airlines both offer this service.

In North America, BWIA and American Airlines fly direct from New York and Miami; Air Canada flies from Toronto and Montreal; Air Jamaica flies from New York, Los Angeles, Atlanta, Chicago and Miami, although passengers have to change planes in Jamaica. American Eagle also flies via its Puerto Rico hub in San Juan.

There are many good and competitively-priced connections from many of the other Caribbean islands with LIAT, British Airways, BWIA, Air Jamaica and Helenair.

Fare Information

In the UK:

British Airways	0345-222111
Virgin Atlantic	01293-747747
Caledonian	01293-535353
BWIA	0181-577-1100
American Airlines	0345 789789
Caledonian	01293 56321

In North America:

BWIA	1-800-327-7401
American Airlines	1-800-433-7300
Air Canada	1-800-776-3000
Air Jamaica	1-800-523-5585
American Eagle	1-800-433-7300

If you plan to visit other islands on your trip, it is worth remembering that tickets purchased in Barbados have VAT added. Try, therefore, to plan your itinerary showing Barbados as a stop-over, even though you may 'stop-over' for a week or two. Prices for inter-island travel with the various airlines are extremely competitive, so shop around for the best deal.

Tour Operators

The best bet for a Caribbean holiday is to put yourself in the hands of a knowledgeable travel agent, who can find the best offer to suit your particular requirements. The best ones should know about combining island hopping side-trips within your main ticket. Most Caribbean holidays are sold as packages, offering different destinations and resorts with the main flights included. The following are a few tour operators specialising in the Caribbean.

In the UK:

Airtours, Wavell House, Holcombe Road, Helmshore, Rossendale, Lancs BB4 4NB. Telephone: 01706-260000

Caribbean Connection, Concorde House, Forest Street, Chester CH1 1QR. Telephone: 01244-341131; Fax: 01244-310-255.

Caribtours, 16, Fulham Road, London SW3 6SN. Telephone: 0171-581-3517; Fax: 0171-225-2491

Elegant Resorts, The Old Palace, Chester CH1 1RB. Telephone: 01244-329671; Fax: 01244-341-084.

Thomas Cook Holidays, PO Box 36, Thorpe Wood, Peterborough, Cambridgeshire PE3 6SB. Telephone: 01733-332255; Fax 01733-505784

Thomson Holidays
Reservations Number 0990-502399

In the USA:

American Express Vacations
Telephone toll free: 1 800-241-1700

Caribbean Concepts
Telephone: 516-496-9800; Fax 516-496-9880

GoGo Tours
Telephone toll free: 1-800-526-0405

Travel Impressions
Telephone toll free: 1-800-284-0044

When To Go

The more popular time to visit is during the dry season which runs from December to May. However, the climate varies very little during the year. Trade winds off the ocean keep humidity to an acceptable level, and although three quarters of the annual rainfall occurs between June and October, the weather is warm throughout the year. Even in the rainy season, downpours are usually short and sharp and everything dries quickly in the hot sun.

Like much of the Caribbean, Barbados may be affected by a hurricane, both directly or by high winds and rain from hurricanes that pass at a distance. Officially, June to November is the season for tropical storms in the Caribbean, but September is regarded as the month at greatest risk.

What to pack

Apart from beachwear (for the beach only!), comfortable and lightweight clothing is all you need with a lightweight jacket or wrap for the occasional cooler evening. Restaurants and hotels expect visitors to change out of their beach or sportswear for dinner and cool and elegantly casual is the usual style.

Barbados offers a wide variety of activities on the island – not all of them on flat surfaces! If you plan to enjoy any of the many sporting or outdoor activities, remember to take appropriate clothing. A good pair of tennis shoes or comfortable closed walking shoes are a must, as are comfortable jeans for horseback riding. Keen bird-watchers should pack a small pair of binoculars.

If you are on regular medication, take supplies with you, but remember that customs authorities can be tough on any prescriptions drugs being brought into the country, so take a copy of your regular prescription to be on the safe side.

As far as photography goes, be self-sufficient. Bring a spare camera battery (or two), and plenty of film. Although film is available on the island, it is not cheap.

Remember to take sunhat, sunglasses, high factor sunscreen, swimsuits, a basic first aid kit (include travel sickness pills, diarrhoea medication and rehydration salts) and plenty of insect repellent. If you wear contact lenses, remember to bring cleaning solutions, as well as a spare set of lenses.

Vaccination and immunisation

Vaccinations are not required unless arriving from an area where a particular disease is endemic; typhoid, poliomyelitis and tetanus are recommended if in doubt. Children's normal vaccinations should be up to date. The biggest plague, however, is the mosquito. While there is no malaria on the island, dengue fever (a flu-like illness with high fever, aches and an irritating rash several days later) is present and is carried by the mosquito. There is no vaccination against the fever – it is advisable to simply try and avoid mosquito bites.

Visa/Immigration Requirements

Valid passports – but no visas – are needed by British citizens, as well as visitors from European Union or Commonwealth countries provided they are not planning to stay for more than ninety days.

If staying for less than six months, North American visitors can enter with just an ID card, but must have a valid return air ticket with them on arrival.

You may be asked to tell the immigration officer where you are staying on the island, and if you do not already hold a reservation, you may have to wait until the officer can give you advice on hotels.

Airline essentials and comfort

The general rule is to have a carry-on bag that is small and light, but provides you with the comforts you need. Always hand carry your passport/visa, airline tickets, traveller's cheques, cash (including some dollars), credit cards, toiletry kit and reading material. It is also a good idea to have your driver's licence, itinerary, water, camera and film with you.

Make a photocopy of your passport and credit cards and keep them in a separate part of your luggage; make sure you know how to cancel your credit cards should they be stolen. It is also advisable to always hand carry valuables like jewellery.

Customs & Excise

Visitors to Barbados are limited to a duty free allowance of:

200 cigarettes *or* 250 grams of tobacco

0.75 litre of spirits

0.75 litre of wine

50 grams of perfume

Other items to a value of Bd$ 100

It is forbidden to import agricultural products, firearms and narcotics. If you have any queries regarding the importation of any goods, check with the Customs Department, Tel: 246-427-5940.

Allowances on leaving Barbados depend on the regulations that apply in your destination.

For the UK, the duty free limits are:

200 cigarettes *or* 100 cigarillos *or* 50 cigars *or* 250 grams of tobacco

One litre of alcohol over 22 per cent vol. *or* two litres of fortified or sparkling wine or other liqueurs plus two litres of still table wine

Fifty grams of perfume and 250ml. of toilet water

UK£145.00 sterling worth of other goods; keep receipts for proof of purchase price

Remember: these allowances are for adults and anyone under the age of seventeen is not entitled to any tobacco or alcohol allowance.

It is prohibited to import *counterfeit* items such as watches, CDs and audio equipment into the UK. Plants, either whole or as seeds, bulbs or cuttings etc. are also illegal. Most animals and birds, except those with a special import licence, are excluded as are certain products made from animals such as ivory, fur and reptile leather goods.

For the USA, the duty free limits are:

200 cigarettes *or* 50 cigars *or* 2kg tobacco

One litre only of alcohol

A reasonable amount of perfume

Goods to a value of US$400

There is an extensive list of other prohibited items including firearms, drugs, obscene publications, and pirated copies of copyrighted works. Plants are banned unless an import permit has been obtained. Food products are subject to conditions prevailing in their country of origin.

Pets such as dogs and cats must be free from any disease that can be passed on to humans. Vaccination against rabies is not required for dogs and cats as long as they are arriving from a rabies-free country.

Further information can be obtained from the US Customs Service, PO Box 17423, Washington DC, 10041; or from the US Embassy, Grosvenor Square, London W1A 2JB.

on arrival

Grantley Adams International Airport

(Tel: 428-7101) is a modern and well-equipped airport, but at the height of the tourist season, between January and April, immigration formalities can take time.

There are *bureau de change* facilities in both the arrivals and departure areas, which are open from 8.00am to midnight. There is also a post office, several car rental agencies and an *in-bound* Duty Free Shop. This can save visitors the trouble of carrying duty-free items all the way from their home country. (See above for allowances).

The airport is about 6 miles (4km) from the capital of Bridgetown. Many visitors prefer to take a taxi to their destination rather than be faced with hiring a car on arrival and driving off into the unknown. There is a large sign in the arrivals area listing the fares in both Barbados and US dollars to various hotels and points around the island.

Airport taxes

There is a departure tax of Bd$25.00 per person to be paid for all destinations whether it be a return flight home, or an island-hopping trip. It is advisable to have the exact amount in local currency, so remember to keep enough at the end of your holiday.

getting around

By air

If you are planning on visiting any other islands, it is worth investing in one of the "island-hopper" tickets offered by LIAT, the largest carrier in the Eastern Caribbean, which flies in and out of Grantley Adams International Airport. The LIAT office is in St. Michael's Plaza, St. Michael's Row in Bridgetown, (Tel: 436-6224). Other inter-island flights are offered by Air Jamaica, (Tel: toll-free 1-800-523-5585); Air Martinique, (Tel: 431-0540); and BWIA, Fairchild Street, Bridgetown, (Tel: 426-2111).

The British Airways head office is located on Fairchild Street, Bridgetown, (Tel: 436-6413). American Airlines are based at the airport, (Tel: 428-4170).

Bajan Helicopters are based at their heliport near the harbour in Bridgetown (Tel: 431-0069) and run various sightseeing tours. (*See Sightseeing Spectacular, page 48*).

By bus

Barbados is justifiably proud of its bus system that fans out across the island from Bridgetown. For routes to the south, buses leave from Fairchild Street; for the northern part of the island, buses start in Lower Green and on Princess Alice Highway. Destinations are indicated by number and not name, so make sure you know which number you need to catch. Buses generally run at fifteen-minute intervals on the main routes. For further information and schedules, Tel: 436-6820. There is a standard fare of Bds$1.50 for any journey regardless of distance. Remember to carry the exact change for the fare. The red and white bus stops are found around the island and are marked either "To City" or "Out of City" depending on whether the bus is heading into or away from Bridgetown!

The government's national bus company of Barbados runs blue buses with yellow stripes, but there are also yellow privately-operated minibuses that cover shorter routes. These have a destination board on the windshield and you pick them up in Bridgetown at River Road, Temple Yard and Probyn Street. The fare is the same – Bds$1.50. Privately owned white mini vans known as route taxis are identified by the ZR on their number plate. They pack in passengers and stop anywhere on route they are flagged down.

By car

If you like your independence it is definitely worth hiring a car. International car rental companies do not operate in Barbados, but the local operators offer an efficient service with well-maintained vehicles. The most recommended firm is **National** on Bush Hall Main Road, St. Michael (Tel: 426-0603). They provide a friendly and helpful service and will deliver vehicles to anywhere around the island, as well as meet visitors on arrival at the airport. They have a good selection of automatic cars, Samurai jeeps, mini-mokes and six-seater vans. Their vehicles are well-maintained and they offer extremely competitive rates.

Other companies are listed in the Yellow Pages and offer a wide selection of vehicles. Also look out for inclusive offers in your holiday and flight package.

Visitors must have a full driving licence with them when they purchase the essential Barbados driving permit for Bds$10.00 at either the main police station in Bridgetown or at the airport on arrival. If requested, the rental company will arrange the permit for you. It is usually cheaper to book a vehicle in advance of your arrival, and also highly recommended during the high season when cars are more difficult to find. You will need a credit card for the security deposit and it is advisable to thoroughly check the vehicle when signing the agreement to confirm that every dent is identified and agreed.

Scooters can be rented from for about US$35.00 a day from **Fun Seekers** in Rockley, Christ Church (Tel: 435-8206). Make sure you wear a helmet and are fully insured. For a more leisurely means of exploring the island, bicycles can be hired from Fun Seekers for about

US$10.00 per day. A deposit is required when hiring both scooters or bicycles.

Driving in Barbados is on the left-hand side of the road. Signs are reasonably good and it is not difficult to find your way around. Keep your eyes open for hand-written signs pointing towards the more interesting and unexplored sights. The speed limit in the towns is 20 mph (32 kph) and in the country it is 37 mph (48 kph). Remember to wear a seat belt all the time.

There are penalties for drinking and driving, as well as illegal parking. Beware of apparently helpful offers (for a small fee) to find you a parking spot – it may not be a legal one!

Petrol stations are open Monday-Saturday from 6.30am-8pm; some are open on Sundays and holidays from 2-6pm. Petrol is not cheap and must be paid for in cash.

By taxi

There are plenty of taxis for hire which are identified by the letter "Z". Although the taxis do not have meters, the rates are fixed by the government, based on a rate of US$16.00 per hour. Drivers are usually helpful, cheerful and honest, and will give a list of standard rates on request. Over-charging is the exception rather than the rule!

In **Bridgetown**, Tel: 426 3337; in **Hastings,** Tel: 427 0240; in **St. James**, Tel: 432 0367 and in

Hastings, Tel: 435 8211. **Co-op Taxis** operate island-wide and can be contacted on 428 0953.

Sightseeing

There are many local companies that offer island-wide sightseeing tours. L.E. Williams Tour Company (Tel: 427-1043) has been established for over twenty-five years and offers excellent day trips to various attractions around Barbados.

Their tours include a coastal island tour; a nature and historical tour; Harrison's Cave tour: Bridgetown historical and shoping tour as well as sailing cruises on the *Why Not*. Their prices are inclusive of entrance fees to the sights. Their helpful staff are also happy to customize tours for visitors and knowledgeable guides know some interesting places away from the beaten track. Tours usually include lunch and drinks.

getting acclimatized

Business hours

Although store hours do vary, in general they are open Monday-Friday from 8.30am-4.30pm; Saturdays 8.30am to 4.00pm. Some stores may close for a lunch hour break. Most are closed on Sunday.

Climate

Barbados' climate, although it is sub-tropical, is claimed to be one of the healthiest in the Caribbean, and

the constant north-west tradewinds keep humidity at an acceptable level. Daytime temperatures range from the low-70s (21°C) to the upper-80s (30°C). The hottest time of the year is June through August, when temperatuares may reach the mid-90s (35°C). The months of February to May are the driest when humidity is at its lowest. The wettest month is July; but even then it unlikely to rain every day.

Being in the Tropics, sunrise and sunset times are fairly constant throughout the year. In summer, the sun rises at around 5.30am and sets around 6.30pm. In winter, sunrise is about an hour later and sunset an hour earlier.

It is difficult to think of the Caribbean without thinking of hurricanes, but at its southerly latitude, Barbados is not often affected by major storms. However, the most likely month for these is September, although the "season" for hurricanes can run from the beginning of June through to the end of November.

If you are unlucky enough to be in Barbados when a hurricane is imminent, follow local advice on when and where to take shelter, and **DO SO**. Do not be foolish enough to think you know better as tropical storms of any magnitude are potentially very dangerous. There is usually enough warning of an impending storm to give visitors the chance to leave if they wish.

Courtesy and respect

Politeness, respect and good manners are an integral part of Caribbean culture in general. Bajans practice this in everyday life, and naturally expect guests to do the same. A smile and warm greeting will go a long way.

Swimwear should be confined to the beach and pool areas. When walking in town, it is polite for men to wear a shirt, and ladies wishing to avoid comments should not wear short shorts. Women who are scantily clad will not be permitted to enter some of the buildings in Bridgetown, including the Parliament Buildings, St. Michael's Cathedral or the Synagogue.

When taking photographs of anybody or a small group of people, it is courteous to ask first. Many Bajans, especially the elderly, harbour mysterious ideas concerning photographs, believing that they can be used in *obeah* spells or will "steal their soul".

If you want to haggle or "discuss" a price, remember that this is a very British-influenced society, so do not try to drive to hard a deal.

Electricity

Barbados is on 110 volts, 50 cycles so American appliances can be used. Dual voltage British items will work satisfactorily; but European appliances will require adapters which most hotels can supply.

Media

The major newspapers in Barbados are *The Barbados Advocate* (daily) which also produces *The Sunday Advocate* and *The Nation* (Monday to Friday), which also published *The Sun on Saturday,* and The *Sunday Sun*. They are all published in English. There is also the useful weekly *Sunseeker* and *The Visitor* which gives current tourist information and entertainment details. *Caribbean Week,* which covers the whole of the Caribbean, is published in Barbados. Overseas newspapers are available at some hotels, news-stands and shops.

Television offerings include broadcasts by the Caribbean Broadcasting Corporation (CBC) on Channel 8 and pay-TV which includes CNN news from 6am to 10am daily.

The radio stations are the public service channel of *Voice of Barbados* (95.3 FM) and CBC (100.1 FM). They carry music and news throughout the day.

Money

There are no currency restrictions in Barbados and the official currency is the Barbados dollar, (Bds$). There are five, ten, twenty, and 100 dollar notes, as well as ten and twenty-five cent silver coins and one and five cent copper coins. The Bajan dollar is worth approximately fifty US cents or forty pence sterling. US dollars and travellers cheques are accepted in the tourist areas, so it is therefore advisable to bring American currency with you. Remember that when someone refers to a dollar, they are usually talking about a Barbados dollar. Always make sure you know which currency you mean when you are negotiating for anything!

It is better to exchange currency at a bank than at a hotel, where you would get five to ten per cent less on the exchange rate. Better rates are also given for cash rather than traveller's cheques. Remember that you need identification, such as your passport, when you change money. It is advisable to keep all receipts of exchange transactions, which you may need to exchange extra local currency back into US dollars or UK sterling on departure.

Banks

Banks are open 8am until 3pm from Monday to Thursday and 8am to 5pm on Friday. The branches of the Caribbean Commercial Bank in the Hastings and Sunset Crest areas are open on Saturday mornings from 9am to 12noon. The branch of the Barbados National Bank at the airport is open every day from 8am until whenever the last flight has arrived or departed. Its *bureau de change* desk is open from 8am to midnight. In addition to main offices in Bridgetown, most of the banks have branches around the island, particularly in the main tourist areas of the south and west coasts.

In a country where financial matters are an expanding part of the economy, there are a several offshore banks, as well as representatives of many of the world's leading financial organizations.

Scotiabank, Bank of Nova Scotia
Broad Street, Bridgetown, tel: 431-3000

Independence Square, Bridgetown, tel: 436-6428

Holetown, St. James's, tel: 432-1662

Haggatt Hall, Julie 'N Complex, tel: 430-3000

Barbados National Bank
Airport Branch, tel: 428-0921

Head Office, Broad Street, Bridgetown, tel: 431-5700

Fairchild Street, Bridgetown tel: 431-5700

Speightstown, tel: 422-4104

Sam Lord's Castle, tel: 423-8210

Barclays Bank plc
Head Office: Broad Street, Bridgetown, tel: 431-5151

Wildey, tel: 431-5458

Speightstown, tel: 422-2194

Oistins, tel: 428-7444

Hilton Hotel, tel: 431-5490

Lower Broad Street, tel: 431-5000

Rendezvous, tel: 431-5430

Sunset Crest, tel: 432 1472

St. Lawrence Gap, tel: 428-7452

Caribbean Commercial Bank
Broad Street, Bridgetown, tel: 431-2500

Mutual Bank of the Caribbean Inc.
Trident House, Lower Broad Street, Bridgetown, tel: 436-8335

Royal Bank of Canada
Main Branch, Broad Street, Bridgetown, tel: 431-6700

Chelston Park, tel: 431-6600

St. Lawrence Gap, tel: 431-6565

Black Rock, tel: 417-1700

Credit Cards
All major credit cards are accepted at Barbados' shops and restaurants – in fact, they are generally preferred by many businesses to traveller's cheques. Most of the banks have ATM machines.

Religion

Although Barbados is predominantly Christian, there are more than a hundred different religious sects in Barbados and, as the saying goes, a church for every day of the year! While some forty per cent of the population are Anglican, there are dozens of other Christian denominations including Roman Catholic. There are also communities of Jews, Muslims and Hindus who all add to the rainbow of powerful religious activity in Barbados. Visitors are welcome to attend services and details of services are published in local newspapers each week.

Sunday mornings are a bustle of activity as congregations, dressed in their smartest and most colourful outfits, head to their chosen places of worship. Little girls look particularly attractive in their matching outfits, while their brothers wear miniature copies of their fathers' Sunday-best suits.

Music is a powerful element in Caribbean religion and combines the traditional ancient & modern with Gospel singing, as well as the native calypso and reggae style.

The *Yellow Pages* of the Barbados Telephone Directory lists most of the religious establishments, from *Abundant Life Assembly* through the *Evangelical Association of the Caribbean* and the *Methodist* and *Moravian Churches* to the *Worldwide Church of God*. There is a long list of Anglican churches, as there are several in each of the eleven parishes of the island. The centre of the Roman Catholic faith is **St. Patrick's Cathedral** off Trafalgar Square in Bridgetown, (Tel: 426-2325).

St. Michael's Cathedral is the centre of the Anglican church and the Church Diocesan Office is at Mandeville House, (Tel: 426-2761).

Post and couriers

The postal service is efficient and airmail post to the UK usually takes between five and six days. The island's main post office is on Cheapside in Bridgetown (Tel: 437-2004). It is open from Monday to

Friday between 7.30am and 5pm. It has poste restante facilities for receiving mail. Post offices can be found in every parish and hours are Monday from 8.00am-noon and 1pm-3.15pm and Tuesday to Friday from 8am-noon and 1pm-3.15pm. There is a Federal Express office at Grantley Adams Airport (Tel: 420-7380) and also in Beckwith Mall on Lower Broad Street, Bridgetown (Tel: 420-7380).

Telephone

The island's telephone system is operated by Bartel, a subsidiary of Cable & Wireless.

The area code for Barbados is 246. To dial a Barbados number from overseas, first dial the international access code, then "246" followed by the Barbados number.

In Barbados, the pay-phone rate is 25 cents for three minutes, but local calls from homes, offices and private residences are free. Hotels may make a charge even for the free local calls and certainly for inter-island and international ones.

Direct-dial overseas and inter-island calls are possible from Barbados, and the connections are generally good, although expensive. It is wise to carry at least two long-distance calling cards such as AT&T, MCI and Sprint because you may experience trouble using some of them. If the operator claims you cannot use your calling card, ask to be put through to an international operator, who can help you. Unless you have money to burn, do not place a long-distance call through your hotel switchboard as some places can add up to a 400 percent surcharge!

You can make international phone calls at the Barbados External Telecommunications office on the Wharf in Bridgetown. Telex and fax facilities are also available at this office.

Phone cards for various amounts can be purchased locally from telephone offices, Cave Shepherd or Super Centre supermarkets. These enable visitors to make calls at cheaper rates.

For operator assistance, dial 0.

Time

Barbados is on North American Eastern Standard Time, five hours behind GMT (four hours behind during daylight savings time. If it is noon in Barbados, it will be 4pm in London, 5pm in Rome and noon in New York.

Tipping

Most hotels and restaurants automatically include between a five and ten per cent service charge on the bill, unless otherwise stated. It is rarely left up to the individual, but you can always leave more if you have enjoyed exceptional service. Some all-inclusive hotels ask that no tips are given and this will be stated in the information pack provided on check-in or at the hotel's welcome sessions. Taxi drivers appreciate a ten per cent tip, while 75US cents per bag is a good rule of thumb for porters and bellhops.

What to buy

Barbados has become the tax free haven of the Eastern Caribbean and as it is is one of the more sophisticated islands in the region, shopping can be a rewarding, as well as an enjoyable experience. Remember to carry your entry card if you plan to buy tax-free goods. You are allowed to take away tax-free goods at the time of purchase, apart from any liquor and tobacco which will be delivered to the airport or port when you leave.

Broad Street in Bridgetown is the main centre for quality stores, notably **Cave Shepherd**, established in 1906 and now an air-conditioned luxury department store. **Dacostas Mall**, also on Broad Street, is situated within an historic listed building and is worth a visit.

Other shopping centres and tax-free shops are scattered around other parts of the island, particularly in the Holetown area, and most of the larger hotels have attractive shops and boutiques. Look out for the work of the talented Bajan designers who produce high quality and stylish clothing that is as comfortable as it is chic. (See *Shopping*, page 110).

There is a huge selection of outlets where attractive mementoes can be purchased. Leather goods, exclusive shell-designs, colourful pottery, original works of art, limited edition prints, and beautiful local craftworks created from the island's most readily-available resources all make excellent souvenirs. Arrangements can be made for shipping the larger, more fragile and expensive items,

An attractive and exclusively Bajan gift is a **Ganzee** T-shirt and the Ganzee shops are to be found all over the island.

The **Cloister Bookshop** on Hincks Street has an excellent selection of books, but if you are looking for the best selection of books on the island, then look no further than the **Best of Barbados Gift Shops**. With fourteen shops scattered around the island, visitors also have easy access to a vast range of reasonably-priced souvenirs including posters, maps, cookbooks, tea towels, tiles, aprons all reflected in the vibrant colours of the Caribbean.

If you are self-catering, there are plenty of bargains to be found at the colourful local markets. Fish, in particular, is sparklingly fresh and cheap. Fresh snapper, mahi-mahi, lobster and crayfish (in season) are reasonably priced and usually available. There are a number of well-stocked supermarkets on Barbados and **Julie's Supermart** in Bridgetown has a great selection of all supplies. They are open from Monday to Thursday from 8am to 9pm and Friday and Saturday from 8am -10pm. There is a village supermarket in Hastings which is open from Monday to Saturday from 8am to 6pm and a **Super Centre** in Oistins which is open from Monday to Saturday from 8am to 8pm. There are several well-stocked supermarkets around the Worthing area and also all along the west coast

What to wear

As the weather is warm all year round because of the tropical climate, summer clothes are the rule; particularly cottons. However, you may need a wrap or sweater during the cooler winter evenings. The general rule for men during the day is casual resort wear, unless one is attending any kind of official function when smarter attire is required. Barbados has some exclusive and elegant restaurants and visitors should dress appropriately when visiting these establishments.

When shopping in town, wear neat shorts or a skirt and a casual top. Swimwear should be reserved for the beach and do not wear it on the street or in town. The same applies to any skimpy clothing. In general, wear cool, comfortable, light-coloured clothing.

staying alive

Health Requirements

Although there are no required vaccinations, Hepatitis A and cholera vaccinations are also sometimes recommended. Although your own doctor is probably up-to-date on vaccinations required for travel to various parts of the world, the latest information can be obtained by contacting the **Center for Disease Control** (CDC) Travellers Hotline in the United States (Tel: 404-332-4559; Fax: 404-332-4565).

The **International Association for Medical Assistance to Travellers** (IAMAT) is another good source for vaccination information to 120 countries. In the USA, contact them on Tel: 716-754-4883 and in Canada on Tel: 519-836-0102. They can be faxed in the US on 519-836-3412. In Europe, IAMAT can be contacted by post at 57 Voirets, 1212 Grand-Lancy-Geneva, Switzerland.

Travel Assistance and Insurance

There is nothing worse than having a medical emergency – or falling ill – when you are on holiday. It is therefore strongly recommended you take out sufficient travel insurance to cover medical treatment, as well as financial investment, luggage and contents replacement. Certain comprehensive policies may also reimburse you for delays due to weather or flight delays.

Check with your own insurance company to see if they can supply insurance either on a short-term or long-term basis. Travel agents can generally arrange something as well, but it pays to compare prices and shop around. Make sure you read the fine print and know what your exclusions are – this is particularly relevant where watersports are concerned. And, importantly, once you have taken out the travel insurance, take a copy of the policy on holiday with you.

There are several well-known organizations, which supply medical policies and trip insurance packages to travellers. One of the largest is **International SOS Assistance**, who have a global referral network of some 2,500 medical professionals and assistance centers staffed around the clock, 365 days a year. They have many offices around the world, including Philadelphia (Tel: 215-244-1500 or 1-800-523-8930; Fax: 215-244-2227). London (Tel: 0181-744-0033), Madrid and Geneva. They also sell medical kits.

There are comprehensive schemes offered in the UK by **American Express** (Tel: 01444-239900); **Trailfinders** (Tel: 0171-938-3939) and **Jardine's** (Tel: 0161-228-3742). In the United States companies offering similar assistance include **Travel Assistance International** (TAI) in Washington, DC (Tel: 1-800-821-2828 or 202-331-1609; Fax: 202-331-1588); **TravMed** in

Baltimore (Tel: 1-800-732-5309 or 410-296-5050; Fax: 410-825-7523) and **US Assist**, also in Washington (Tel: 202-537-7340).

Beat the Heat

It pays to remember that Barbados is in the "Tropical Zone" – the area that straddles the equator. This means that the sun is much stronger here than at home.

Do not be fooled – although the cool breezes will feel soothing as you lie on that beach, you are steadily baking – think lobster! If you do not want to end up bearing a striking resemblance to this aforementioned crustacean – and experience the pain and discomfort that is guaranteed to come with sunburn – it is advisable to always remember a few things:

Avoid the midday sun (even if you are an Englishman or a mad dog). Give yourself half-an-hour in the sun in the morning, and another half hour in the late afternoon. Clouds do NOT protect against UV rays. You will still get burned if you are not careful. Look for a high SPF when choosing your sun lotion – and try to ensure it is water-resistant. If not, reapply after each time you have been in for a swim.

Remember that water reflects the sun's rays so if you are sitting beside the pool, or on the beach, you are experiencing a double dose

of strong sun. The glare will also affect you and can cause severely unpleasant headaches.

Always wear strong sunglasses and a broad-brimmed hat. Don't be ashamed to cover up when you need to! If you are starting to turn pink today, then it is likely you will be as red as a beet tomorrow. Snorkellers, in particular, should beware of burning their backs: a long T-shirt – and even lightweight trousers if need be – will help avoid the problem.

Water, water, and more water. And that means drink it, not just swim in it! The sun does more than burn; it dehydrates. So drink water as often as possible; every thirty minutes to one hour is recommended. Avoid sugary drinks and use salt on your food to rehydrate your system.

You will recognize the onset of heat stroke by the following symptoms: your skin is red, hot and dry; your body temperature is high; you are confused mentally and you lose co-ordination. If this should occur seek medical help immediately

If you are trying to assist a heat-stroke victim, you should move them into a cooler location and remove their clothing. You should then fan them and cover them with cold wet cloths until help arrives.

Remedies for Sunburn

Calamine lotion applied to the skin – bring some with you, just in case. Liberally apply aloe, either the gel or sap straight from the leaf of the plant or commercial products

A mixture of two-thirds water and one-third vinegar, applied to the skin

Take aspirin regularly which will help reduce the inflammation.

Tropical Diseases & Cautions

Dengue fever: Yet another disease carried by that scourge of Mother Nature – the mosquito (in particular, *aedes aegypti*). Dengue fever can be hard to detect, because its symptoms are similar to flu: high fever, joint pain, headaches – but also an irritating rash several days later. There is no treatment for this disease so try to avoid getting bitten. Use repellents and wear trousers and long-sleeved shirts when the mosquitoes are most prolific at dawn and dusk. If you get the disease, drink plenty of liquids, take pain killers *acetaminophen* (not aspirin) and rest. Unfortunately, about a year after having dengue fever, some people can develop hemorrhagic dengue: high fever, rapid pulse, measles-like spots and vomiting. If you get these symptoms, see a tropical diseases doctor immediately for treatment.

Venereal disease is prevalent in the Caribbean; including HIV, so remember the dangers of casual sex. Always check that properly sterilised or disposable needles are used should you require urgent medical attention.

Montezuma's Revenge

Well, no one wants to talk about it, but the sad fact is that many of us get it when we travel to an exotic destination: the dreaded diarrhoea. It is generally caused by viruses, bacteria or parasites contained in contaminated food or water. When in doubt about the condition of the water, used bottled and ensure it is sealed and don't ask for ice in your drinks – ice is made from local water!

Make sure hot foods are cooked properly and cold foods have been kept cold. Peel fruit and vegetables before eating them. Avoid eating prepared food from roadside stands unless you are sure it has been kept at constant temperatures.

If you are still unlucky enough to be taken ill, there are a few things you can do. If it is a serious case, seek medical attention immediately. Otherwise, take Pepto Bismol (*bismuth subsalicylate*), which slows down the process, but still lets it run its course. Avoid taking Imodium (*ioperamide*) unless you absolutely have to as it totally blocks up the digestive tract and locks in infections. Certainly do not take it for more than three days.

The best treatment is rest, plenty of fluids and salt replacement. The best antibiotic for bacterial types of travellers' diarrhoea is *ciproflaxicin*. Take regular small portions of bland fluids – ginger ale, flat cola and salty chicken broth are all effective. Try to avoid getting dehydrated, which can be dangerous, especially for young children. It is advisable to carry oral rehydration packets with you. Alternately drink either bottled water or flat cola mixed with some sugar or honey and a pinch of salt or a little baking soda.

Nature's Nasties

As the mongoose put paid to the poisonous snakes on the island, there is only one creepy-crawly to be avoided. The easily recognisable **centipede,** with its segmented reddish-brown body and many legs, can give the unwary visitor a poisonous bite. Fortunately, centipedes inhabit unattractive places such as piles of rubbish, rotting vegetation, and derelict structures, so it is unlikely that any, but the most unlucky will encounter this creature. If you do see one, do not try to touch it.

Hiking during the dry season – December through April – may also bring unpleasant encounters with chiggers – mites which live in the grass, and pierce or burrow into the skin, leaving hard nodules and a small bumpy red rash at the point of entry. "Chigger Guard" is an excellent treatment; but even fingernail polish dabbed on the bites can be effective.

Some of the terrestrial flora can be equally unpleasant. Certain trees and plants should be admired only from a safe distance such as the

manchineel tree, which grows in coastal areas. This is a medium-sized tree with bright green and glossy ovate leaves. Its green fruit resembles crab apples. Both the sap and the apples are toxic and can cause severe skin blistering. For this reason many are marked with a red band painted around the trunk. Do not take shelter under them when it rains, as the sap is toxic when mixed with water. The Caribs originally used the sap to poison their arrow tips.

The prolific and beautiful **oleander** is often used as a border for gardens and lawns; its usually pink flowers look much like the mountain laurel. The wood from this plant is extremely toxic and should not be burned – so if you have any impromptu barbecues, avoid this willowy plant. All other parts of the oleander are also poisonous, so it is advisable to steer well clear of it.

Marine menaces include young **Portuguese men-of-war**, which sometimes visit the Atlantic coast beaches. Generally light blue or pink in colour, tinged with purple, they appear to be tiny bubbles of plastic floating in the water, trailing a few thready tentacles. They can give nasty rope-like stings, which are painful but not dangerous. You can even get stung if you step on one that has been washed up on the beach, so tread with care. Tea tree oil applied directly to the affected area offers some relief.

Personal Security & Safety

Common sense should prevail here and like anywhere else in the world, you must be careful.

Do not wear ostentatious jewellery, dress sensibly, lock up your valuables, carry only small amounts of cash, always lock your car doors, don't wander in deserted streets or on the beach late at night, don't go out alone, and keep hold of your purse at all times. Avoid unlit or unpatrolled areas at night, and in particular the red-light district of Bridgetown. Seek local advice on what other areas to avoid. If you do get robbed, don't try to be a hero just give them what they want and don't argue. Immediately contact your hotel security and local police.

If you are driving, don't stop if you are flagged down, no matter how callous that may seem. Don't make something that is not your problem become your problem. And never pick up hitchhikers.

You will probably encounter street hawkers and peddlers on the beach. Drugs, in particular are illegal and an increasing problem on Barbados. Marijuana and crack cocaine use is widespread and is often distributed on south coast beaches. If you do not want to be bothered, the best rule is to say, politely but firmly, "no thanks". On the street, it is easy: just keep on walking. On the beach it may not be that simple. If anybody persists or get increasingly obnoxious, remove yourself and find another spot.

Emergencies:

Police, dial 112

Fire, dial 113

Air/Sea Rescue, dial 427 8819

Ambulance Service, dial 115

The police headquarters is at Black Rock, Bridgetown and there are police stations at the airport and in most of the other parish centres.

Hospitals

The main hospital on the island is the **Queen Elizabeth Hospital** on Martindale Road, Bridgetown, Tel: 436-6450. There are several more hospitals around the island, including:

The private **Bayview Hospital** on St. Paul's Avenue, Tel: 436-5446

Christ Church District Hospital Tel: 428-9001

Gordon Cummins Hospital Tel: 432-1130

St. Lucy Hospital Tel: 439-8424

St. Philip Hospital Tel: 423-7311.

There are also out-patients clinics in each Parish.

There is a **decompression chamber** unit operated by the Barbados Defence Force in the Garrison area of Bridgetown. Tel: 436-6185.

Dentists

There are a number of reliable dental surgeries on the island, including:

Beckwith Dental Services in Beckwith Mall, Bridgetown. Tel: 426-3001

Family Dental Clinic at 7 Rickett Street, Bridgetown. Tel: 228 1759

Pine Dental Services offers a twenty-four-hour emergency service (Bleeper No. 3368) Tel: 436-1420

Your hotel can also refer a local dentist if necessary.

Pharmacies

Cheapside Pharmacy in Bridgetown. Tel: 437-2004. They are open from Monday to Friday from 7.30am to 5.30pm and on Saturday from 7.30am to 1.30pm.

Collin's in Broad Street, Bridgetown. Tel: 426-4515 or in Speightstown Tel: 422-5319

Holborn Pharmacy, Pine Road, St. Michael. Tel: 430-0540

Lewis's Drug Mart in Christ Church. Tel: 435-8090. They are open from Monday to Friday from 9am to 6pm, Saturday 9am to 1pm and Sunday from 9am to noon.

Knight's Pharmacy, Oistins, Tel: 436-6120 is open from Monday to Saturday from 8am to 8pm and Sunday from 8am to 1pm.

tourist information

Barbados

The head office for The Barbados Tourism Authority is in Bridgetown on Harbour Road.

Address all correspondence to The Barbados Tourism Authority PO Box 242, Harbour Road, Bridgetown, Barbados, West Indies Tel: 246-427-2623/2624 Fax: 246-426-4080)

There is another tourism office at the Sherbourne Centre, Two Mile Hill in Saint Michael. Tel: 430-7500.

There are also information offices at Grantley Adams International Airport (Tel: 428-7101) and the Port of Bridgetown (Tel: 426-1718).

Barbados Tourism Offices overseas

United Kingdom
1 Great Russell Street, London WC1B 3NH Tel: 0171-636-9448/9449 Fax: 0171-637-1496 *website address*: http://www.barbados.org.uk

Canada
105 Adelaide Street West, Suite 1010, Toronto, Ontario M5H 1P9 Tel: 416-214-9880 Fax: 416-268-9122

Germany
Neue Minazxer Strasse 22, D-603-11, Frankfurt am Main Tel: 069-23-23-66 Fax: 069-23-00-77

France
c/o Tropic Travel, 8-10 rue Saint Marc, Paris Tel: 1-42-36-51-18 Fax: 1-42-36-51-19

United States of America
800 Second Avenue, New York, NY 10017 Tel: 212-986-6516/8 Toll-free: 1-800-221-9831 Fax: 212-573-9850

Embassies and Consulates

British High Commission
British High Commission Building, Lower Collymore Street, St. Michael, Tel: 436-6694 Fax: 436-5398

Canadian High Commission
Bishop's Court Hill, St. Michael Tel: 429-3550

French Consulate
Waverley House, Hastings, Christ Church Tel: 435-6847

Italian Vice Consulate
Bannatyne Plantation, Christ Church Tel: 437-1228

Netherlands Consulate
Chickmont Foods Barbados Ltd, Balls Plantation, Christ Church Tel: 418-8074

Embassy of the Republic of China
17 Golf View Terrace, Rockley, Christ Church Tel: 435-6890, Fax: 435-8300

Embassy of the United States of America
Canadian Imperial Bank Building, Broad Street, Bridgetown Tel: 436-4950, Fax: 429-5316

index